Black-on-Black VIOLENCE

THE PSYCHODYNAMICS OF BLACK SELF-ANNIHILATION IN SERVICE OF WHITE DOMINATION

AMOS N. WILSON

AFRIKAN WORLD INFOSYSTEMS
NEW YORK 1990

Typesetting and editing by Sababu N. Plata

Cover illustration by Joe Gillians

ISBN 1-879164-00-0

AFRIKAN WORLD INFOSYSTEMS
256 East 138 Street
Bronx, New York 10451

AFRIKAN WORLD INFOSYSTEMS
743 Rogers Avenue, Suite 6
Brooklyn, New York 11226

Printed in the U.S.A.

DEDICATION

To

My Brothers and Sisters in Struggle

Acknowledgments

I extend my heartfelt thanks to Sababu Plata whose extra-ordinary patience, proofreading, editorship, logistical support, feedback and whose endless hours of word-processing made the typesetting of this manuscript a reality.

I commend Robert and Willette Dobson whose gentle prodding, unwavering faith in my work, and financial support made the printing and promotion of this book possible.

Sincere thanks to the Joseph family, Margaret, Kwame and Akuya, H. Celestine whose ready investment and trust in this undertaking pushed us uphill and over the hump.

Appreciation to Charles Ritzberg, former colleague in the New York City department of probation, and Professor Tutu, for critically proofreading and commenting on the manuscript.

My indebtedness to Yolanda Hernandez, for lending an ever-attentive ear to my many hours of vocal ruminations on the subject matter of this book, for proofreading and commenting on the manuscript, for her unstinting psychological and material support of my aspirations.

To Rosa Plata, for her silent support and for keeping the home fires burning.

Last but not least, my gratitude to the unnamed others who appeared briefly to lend a hand.

Other Books by AMOS N. WILSON

The Developmental Psychology of the Black Child

Awakening the Natural Genius of Black Children

Understanding Black Adolescent Male Violence:
Its Remediation and Prevention

The Falsification of Afrikan Consciousness
*Eurocentric History, Psychiatry and the
Politics of White Supremacy*

Blueprint For Black Power (working title)

About the Author

Professor AMOS N. WILSON is a former social caseworker,
supervising probation officer, psychological counselor, training
administrator in New York City Department of Juvenile Justice,
and Assistant Professor of psychology at the City University
of New York. He is currently Adjunct Professor at The School
of New Resources, College of New Rochelle, Co-op City Campus,
Bronx, New York.

CONTENTS

Contents

Contents

The Battle Must Be Joined !!!

No nation, no civilization has come to the fore
    Without new organization
Without thinking new thoughts
    Without working
Without actually doing
    Without being willing to take a chance
A willingness to risk all
    Without a willingness to go against overwhelming odds
Without a determination to be the best, to be superior
    Without a desire to determine its destiny and that of others
Without a willingness to fight, to shed blood, to risk defeat

The battle must be joined ...

    It must be fought
Be it a battle of mind, mind wars of spirit,
    Of will, of bucks, of iron and steel, shell and bomb
Of tank and plane, of rockets and satellite star wars
    Of technology, of information

The battle must be fought
    The gauntlet thrown down
The chip knocked from the bully's shoulder
    The lines stepped over
The clash and clang of sword
    curses of men, moans of pain

The battle must be joined ...

Fought in the street from door to door
    In the schoolroom, in the board room
In the bedroom, in the war room

Hand to hand combat must commence
The battle must be ultimately won in the field

It matters not if you can eruditely delineate the subtleties
    and nuances of racism, and racial discrimination
If you can delicately dissect with a master surgeon's skill
    the anatomy of race and the body politic
If you can tease out the tiniest thread
    If you can paint the most beautiful dreams on canvas
And write the greatest vision of parchment
    Or ride in your time machine and visit ancient
Afrikan kingdoms, cities, and empires
    Or feel the pain and degradation of slavery
Or celebrate all we have given to the world
    Or point out with great exclamation the white Devil

Still the challenge must be taken up
    Fire must fight fire
Institutions, traditions, habits, hopes must be uprooted,
    razed and put to the torch
No stone left upturned
    And institutions, traditions, habits, hopes must be
restored, rekindled or rebuilt anew
    Bricks stacked in place
New songs must be sung
    New voices must carry the tune
New feet must march to new drumbeats
    New hands, new banners and standards raised

These songs must be your songs
    The voices your voices, the feet your feet
The hands must be the ones at the ends of your arms
    The soul unsold to the devil must be your soul

A new world must be created
Make it your world

Amandla!

INTRODUCTION

THE STATISTICS ARE ALARMING. According to the Uniform Crime Reports, published by the Federal Bureau of Investigation, in 1986 Blacks accounted for 46.5% of all arrests for violent crimes even though Blacks comprised 12% of the U.S. population. Blacks accounted for 48% of the persons arrested for murder; 46.6% of all arrests for rape; 39.8% for assault. In the cities of the United States Blacks accounted for 49.5% of all arrests for violent crimes, e.g., murder, forcible rape, robbery, and aggravated assault. In 1986, of those persons under 18 years of age, Blacks accounted for 54.9% of those arrested for violent crimes. The highest violent crime rates are demonstrated by young Black males. More young Black men died from homicide in one year (1977) than died in ten years in the Vietnam War. Black men are six times as likely as White men to be murder victims. Murder is the fourth leading cause of death for Black males of age 20 to 29. Between the ages of 15 and 24, homicide is the leading cause of death among Black males. The odds of becoming a murder victim are less than one in twenty for young Black males living in the cities, between ages 20 and 29. Most violent crimes (84%) against Blacks were committed by Black offenders.[1] Over 40% of all jail inmates throughout the nation are Black — and the percentage is rapidly rising.

According to political scientist and sociologist, Manning Marable, by 1982 nearly one-half of all suicides among Blacks occurred among people between ages 20 and 34 years. Black males who kill themselves account for 36% of the total number of suicides.[2]

But statistics do not tell the half of it.

---

[1] Brown, Lee. The National Urban League *The State of Black America 1988*

[2] *African Commentary Magazine* May, 1990.

These statistics represent more than the oft-noted outcome of "institutional racism." The violent and self-destructive demise of very significant portions of the African American community, and perhaps the whole of that community, as evidenced by the crime statistics cited above is not merely symptomatic of the socioeconomic ills which plague the lower strata of its social hierarchy. The major, and by far more important part of the story as represented by these statistics, is that the tragic activities they depict are the reactionary result of a deliberate psycho-political campaign against the African American and Pan-African communities. How this is accomplished, and for what reasons, comprise the subject matter of this book.

Statistics can only faintly reflect the psychosocial and socioeconomic turmoil prevalent in far too many inner-cities today. Moreover, they too mutely herald the social Armageddon and Final Judgment fast approaching the African American and worldwide African communities if they do not issue an urgent call to arms and defeat the enemy at their gates.

Well-meaning sociologists and criminologists would have us think that it is unemployment, lack of adequate education and job skills, broken homes, drug addiction, learning disabilities, lack of government commitment, Black male irresponsibility, capitalism (*that beloved psychopolitical straw man of White radicals and Black socialists*), which are among the major causes of Black criminality and Black-on-Black violence. The White American community would have us think that increased police surveillance, apprehension and punishment, increased investment in police weaponry and manpower, increased prison construction (according to Manning Marable, authorities would have to add 1,800 new prison beds *each week*, just to keep pace with the rate of increase in the penal population), longer and harsher sentences, containment of the Black community, "just say no to drugs," "a war on drugs," "a war on poverty," and the like, would curtail or prevent self-destructive violence, criminality, and social deterioration so prevalent in the African American community. Time and experience have amply demonstrated that such approaches are overworked, ineffective and bankrupt. Moreover, such approaches have not attacked the primary causal factor in Black criminality and violence — *White supremacy*.

Introduction

White supremacy by its very nature and intent requires the continuing oppression and subordination of African peoples and, in time, may require their very lives. Subordination of a people requires that that people in some way or ways be violated, dehumanized, humiliated, and that some type of violence be perpetrated against them. The violently oppressed react violently to their oppression. When their reactionary violence, their retaliatory or defensive violence, cannot be effectively directed at their oppressors or effectively applied to their self-liberation, it then will be directed at and applied destructively to themselves. This is the essence of Black-on-Black violence. Oppressive violence is both pro-active and re-active, directed and misdirected. Black men kill each other because they have not yet chosen to challenge and neutralize on every front the widespread power of White men to rule over their lives.

The bane of the African community is the exploitative White American community which projects a so-called civilized, fraternal, egalitarian, liberal face while concurrently seeking to maintain White supremacy. This means that the White American community must maintain African subordination while not appearing to do so. It must cannibalistically sacrifice the vitality, autonomy, and if need be, the life of the African American community while posing as its benefactor and savior. It pleads innocence while washing its hands of the blood of African people. This duplicitous task can only be accomplished by making it appear that the African community is dying of natural causes, not of an ingenious attempt on the part of the White American community to strangle it to death. This means that African American hands must be used to plunge White American-manufactured daggers into the hearts of African American citizens. This is the assigned role of the Black-on-Black violent criminal. How this role is played out will be delineated in the chapters that follow.

To explain the problem of African subordination in terms of racism, racial hatred, and the like, is to misdirect and mislead the African community down the irrational and destructive path of seeking to overcome "racism" (as if "racism" could exist without some *race* of people being empowered to practice it) while leaving the power (and need) to practice this behavior in White hands.

BLACK-ON-BLACK VIOLENCE

The African American and worldwide African communities have chased phantom explanations and solutions to their detriment. While the explanations and solutions expressed in this book may or may not be accepted by the reader, he or she must accept the fact that new explanations and solutions must be found and applied full speed ahead!

At the center of any explanation of violence in the Black American community must exist a detailed description of the conscious and subliminal psychological/material means by which hostile White American hegemonic attitudes are violently acted-out in African American interpersonal relations. Central to any set of solutions to the problems of crime and violence must exist an effective program for curtailing and rendering ineffective the White American community's ability to practice White supremacy, and to continue its domination, benevolent or otherwise, of African American community life. Additionally, the African American community must so construct its psychopolitical consciousness, its socioeconomic relations, the socialization and education of its children, and its cultural values such that it will no longer permit certain of its segments to be unwittingly recruited to execute against its own body politic, White American death-wishes towards it.

We recognize that unemployment, underemployment, poverty, drugs, poor education, inadequate housing, overcrowding and the like, are tangibly *related* to Black-on-Black criminality and violence. We question their casual roles, however. They represent secondary effects. They reflect the fact that White Americans at this time possess an inordinate amount of power to defend and extend their economic, psychopolitical, and sociocultural advantages at the expense of African Americans. These advantages such as they are, can only be enhanced and maintained through racist policies and practices, the current White American pretense of accepting racial integration and assimilation notwithstanding.

Instead of being a remnant from the past, the social hierarchy based on race is a critical component in the organization of modern American society. The subordination because of the color of one's skin is a primary determinant of people's position

xiv

in the social structure. Racism is the structural relationship based on the subordination of one racial group by another. Given this perspective, the determining feature of race relations is not prejudice towards blacks, but rather the superior position of whites and the institutions — ideological as well as structural — which maintain it.[3]

White American power is utilized to spawn the pre-conditions and conditions of Black-on-Black violence. White American politicoeconomic power has been and is utilized to strip the African American community of its power to defend itself against the plagues of violence, drug abuse, crime, AIDS, and other social/biological ailments which so painfully afflict it. This disempowerment of the Black community, the primary purpose of which is to leave it fundamentally defenseless against White American socioeconomic incursion and exploitation, also leaves it defenseless against the other ills which threaten to totally undermine its health and well-being.

Thus, the conditions which are baneful to the African American community are those conditions which help to maintain White American power and domination over that community. These conditions are so subtly orchestrated that their orchestration is often unnoticed by its intended victims, and are, more often than not, misperceived and misinterpreted by them as originating endemically from their own minds and characters. We argue herein that Black-on-Black criminality and violence play a crucial role in maintaining White American power in all of its manifestations.

A sense of powerlessness and interpersonal violence are inextricably intertwined. Absolute powerlessness as well as absolute power, corrupts.

For violence has its breeding ground in impotence and apathy. True, aggression has been so often and so regularly escalated into violence that anyone's discouragement and fear of it can

---

[3] Wellman, D. *Portraits of White Racism*. Cambridge: Cambridge University Press, 1977.

be understood. But what is *not* seen is that the state of powerlessness, which leads to apathy and which can be produced by the above plans for the uprooting of aggression, is the source of violence. As we make people powerless we promote their violence rather than its control. Deeds of violence in our society are performed largely by those trying to establish their self-esteem, to defend their self-image, and to demonstrate that they, too, are significant. Regardless of how derailed or wrongly used these motivations may be or how destructive their expression, they are still the manifestation of positive interpersonal needs. We cannot ignore the fact that, no matter how difficult their redirection may be, these needs themselves are potentially constructive. Violence arises not out of superfluity of power but out of powerlessness. As Hannah Arendt has so well said, violence is the expression of impotence.[4]

Black-on-Black criminality and violence represent quests for power and outraged protests against a sense of powerlessness and insignificance. They are protective fetishes used to defend against feelings of helplessness and vulnerability.

Black-on-Black violence is reflective of vain attempts to achieve basic, positive human ends in a negative environment, by negative means. It represents an often misguided, furious struggle for self-affirmation by many African Americans while entangled in a White American-spun spider's web specifically designed and constructed to accomplish their dis-affirmation. Black-on-Black violence and criminality are rooted in "positive" White American values — irrational quests for power, prestige, possession, affection, and acceptance among peers so as to secure illusory reassurances against anxiety, self-contempt, and feelings of inferiority. They are rooted as well in attempts to protect against exploitation by others also caught up in the same rapacious social environment generated and sustained by egregious White American values.

For too many African American youth, being cut off from the paths to legitimate and self-determined personal accom-

---

[4] May, R. *Power and Innocence: A Search for the Sources of Violence.* N.Y.: W.W. Norton & Co., 1972.

plishment as a result of the underdeveloped power of the African American community, the violent subduing of others may often be their only significant achievement and "claim to fame." They may, as argued by Cloward and Ohlin:

> seize upon the manipulation of violence as a route to status not only because it provides a way of expressing pent-up angers and frustrations but also because they are not cut off from access to violent means by vicissitudes of birth. In the world of violence, such attributes as race, socioeconomic position, age, and the like are irrelevant; personal worth is judged on the basis of qualities that are available to all who would cultivate them. The acquisition of status is not simply a consequence of skill in the use of violence or of physical strength but depends, rather, on one's willingness to risk injury or death in the search for "rep."[5]

The capacity to perpetrate violence is the great equalizer in a world characterized by great inequalities.

The need of many Black males to achieve power and self-affirmation through the use of violence is cogently stated by Coser when he argues that:

> ...in disorganized urban areas of American cities, men tend to feel that only prowess in interpersonal violence or in aggressive sexual encounters allows the achievement of personal identity and permit gaining otherwise unavailable deference. Where no social status can be achieved through socioeconomic channels it may yet be achieved in the show of violence among equally deprived peers.

Coser further notes that:

> Since negroes are assigned the lowest position in all three dimensions of the American status system — ethnicity, class, and education — and since their mobility chances are nil in

---

[5] Cloward R., & Ohlin, L. *Delinquency and Opportunity*. New York: The Free Press, 1965.

the first and minimal in the second and third, it stands to reason that achievement in the area of interpersonal violence might be seen as a channel leading to self-regard and self-enhancement — at least as long as conflict with the dominant white majority seems socially unavailable as a means of collective action.[6]

If we are to curb Black-on-Black crime and violence we must choose to see their presence and increase in ways other than as signals for an all-out "war against crime" (*read*: "war against Black youth, Black males, and the Black community"). Black-on-Black violence and criminality must not be perceived as mere calls to arm a police-state, as the basis for rationalizing increased prison construction and the defensive perception of all Black males as criminals.

These reactionary measures only exacerbate the problem. When will White America (with some very significant proportion of Black America) come to its senses and recognize the various equations it has written on the blackboard of American society? — more police = more crime; more judges = more convicts; more prisons = more inmates; more laws = more criminals; more White repressive violence = more Black reactive violence; more White violence against Black minds = more Black violence against White (and Black) bodies.

The equations must be re-written; new balances must be achieved. And the new equations must include new and equal balances of African American and White American power, prosperity, respect, and positive self-regard.

The constant increase in Black-on-Black violence and criminality reflects the constant incremental generation by prevailing socioeconomic conditions of Black hostility and anxiety fueled by a constantly increasing sense of futility. Thus Black-on-Black violence and criminality are danger signals, flashing red indicators of explosive social inequalities, dysfunctionalities, dislocations, and conflicts. They are alarming reminders that

---

[6] Coser, L. *Continuities in the Study of Social Conflict*. New York: The Free Press, 1967.

Introduction

the White American-dominated body politic is *dis*eased, in danger of cardiac arrest, and in need of radical surgery and intensive care.

More than danger signals to White America, Black-on-Black violence and criminality are calls for the radical self-reconstruction and self-empowerment of the African American community. Consequently, the African American community must wrest control over its material and nonmaterial life from non-African hands if it is to rid itself of intracommunal/interpersonal violence. The demise of Black-on-Black violence will begin with the renaissance of *authentic* Black power.

When we speak of African American/Pan-African self-empowerment we refer not to the bogus, illusory "power" of token Black house-servants, the mock White "power" of the Black bourgeoisie, or the sycophantic, bootlicking, "power" of Black politicians. We neither include the pie-in-the-sky, White God-fearing "power" of Black preachers; the oleaginous diplomatic "power" of puppeted, neocolonial African "heads-of-state," powers which needs ask the permission or authorization of any other race to express and actualize themselves; nor the reactionary, self-destroying, community decimating "power" of the Black-on-Black criminal! We speak here of a true and honest African American/Pan-African Power which springs full-force from African manhood, womanhood and humanity: a power which harnesses the abundant intellectual, emotional, behavioral, cultural, spiritual and material resources of African peoples and uses them to secure and protect the survival, well-being and self-actualization of the total African community. This power we seek will not be given: it must be taken. This is the moment of truth. The African American/Pan-African community must do — or die!

Amos N. Wilson

Note: It is important to note that this book does not purport to offer an explanation of "Black crime" or of the "Black criminal." It is mainly concerned with the psychological and political mechanisms by which a measurable minority of Black Americans is induced to interact violently with each other — in ways which threaten their vital interests and survivability — by the White American community's need to maintain socioeconomic supremacy.

Black-on-Black violence refers to the assaultive, homicidal and suicidal violence committed by Blacks against Blacks in ways that are self- and mutually destructive, egregious and gratuitous. That is, violence committed by Blacks against Blacks which may be classified as "over-reactive," "excessive," "deadly," "senseless," "sadistic," "unprovoked," or rationally not justified by its alleged cause(s); and more importantly, that violence which appears in disproportionately large part to be motivated by the African ethnicity of both the aggressor and the victim and the psychology associated with what it means to be Black under White domination.

Editor's Note

If view of evolving proficiency in publishing technology *Black-on-Black Violence* has been enhanced to take advantage thereof. Those in possession of previous copies will find changes print quality, font selection and page numbering, however the content is identical but for minor grammatical and stylistic changes.

Sababu N. Plata

1

THE SOCIOPOLITICAL NECESSITY

OF BLACK CRIMINALITY

> I would maintain, that some of those conditions which we facilely regard as problematic (and by implication, those which nearly everyone would like to remedy) may nevertheless be *necessary* conditions in American life. Put another way, while these conditions may be troublesome — they certainly injure many people — their existence is culturally mandated and they are intrinsic to the very essence of American society.
>
> — MICHAEL LEWIS
> *The Culture of Inequality*

Most commentators, expert and nonexpert, who purport to explain the vicissitudes of criminality begin with the *a priori* assumption that criminal behavior, by definition and nature, is antisocial. That is, that criminals as deviants, and the criminal activities they perpetrate in service to their own self-centered ends, are determined to seriously derange the peace and orderly functioning of society, to do grievous harm to the lives and liberties of its law-abiding members, and in some instances, to destroy them. Criminals and criminality together are seen as constituting an alien and malignant cancerous growth, invading,

1

attacking, and eating away the vital substance of the benign body politic.

The unexamined assumption that criminality and criminal activity are initiated and sustained by a distinct outlaw class of criminal personalities who are at war against a society of innocent, decent, normal persons, while beguilingly simple and direct is nevertheless disingenuous. Purported criminal types or classes, degrees or levels of criminal activities, as well as the social strata or groups and individuals who perpetrate, aid and abet criminal activities, functionally vary across time and cultures. This pointedly indicates that criminals and criminality, however they may be measured or described, are sociocultural products. They carry and express the sociogenetic inheritance of their societal progenitor. Crime and society are blood relatives. They are intimately and inextricably related.

[Criminal personalities, like all personalities, are to a significant degree socially created and defined. Their behavioral characters can only be manifested within a social context. They therefore cannot stand outside social time, place, and circumstance. When a society collectively looks into the faces of its criminals it looks in a mirror and sees a reflection of its own likeness.]

As the nature of societies change so does the nature of their epiphenomenal criminality and the behavioral personalities of their criminal constituents. Neither criminality nor criminal personalities can exist in the absence of a social milieu.

Criminality as Social Symptom

Criminality may heuristically be perceived as a sociological symptom of a society, not unlike an obsessive-compulsion may be considered a psychological symptom of an individual. It may furthermore be perceived, in the classical Freudian sense, as a maladjustive compromise between two or more conflicting forces within a social or societal personality which have not yet been completely integrated. Criminality as a societal symptom represents a compromise between forces and needs in opposition; forces repressive and repressed, defensive and offensive, oppressive and oppressed, both seeking overt expression and satisfaction. Criminality, as a symptom, is connotative of societal imbalances; of internal sociological incompatibilities; of mutually exclusive inflations and deflations; of social needs being denied and distorted. Symptomatic criminality while reflective of the societal whole, is incarnated and actualized in the minds and bodies of its individual and group constituents. It is emblematic of the societal misallocation of power, energy, and resources; of societal hypocrisy; of a societal refusal to know itself and be true to its reality and possibilities. Criminality, as symptom, is inherently two-faced. It is both conservative and disruptive, enthroning and overthrowing. It serves two masters. It is a double-agent, both serving and betraying.

[Psychoanalytically speaking, criminality as a societal neurotic symptom does not necessarily affect all segments of a society in the same way. For some there are gains, both primary and secondary, and for others losses. The criminal activities of one or more segments of a society may be used by other segments to achieve identity, dominance, wealth and prestige. These dominant societal segments, classes, or groups, are often born and bred of the process of repression and impoverishment of the alienated, "criminal" segments or constituents in their social domain. Addicted to the advantages derived from their oppression of the alienated groups, the dominant groups come to depend, whether consciously or unconsciously acknowledged, on such repressive processes as necessary to their continuing relatively peaceful and profitable existence. Their dominance and advantages more often than not, rests on the deprivational subordination of the other societal elements.]

The primary gain achieved by the dominant class of a society through its repression, denial, distortion, deprivation, and provocation to self-destructive anger its repressed elements, is the creation and enjoyment of a relatively conflict-free, anxiety-free, guilt-free, secure existence buttressed by a tenuous autonomy and control of its environment. Secondary gains may include apparent self-preservation, avoidance of responsibility for the state of its repressed elements, material advantages, attention and respect, increased control and influence over other people and the environment, as well as enhancement of its self- and social-image. It is to the greater glory of the ruling classes, that dominant class of classes — regulator of the societal economy, center of societal consciousness and self-consciousness, producer and protector of the societal self- and public image, guardian and keeper of the self-serving peace, law and order — that a societal symptom such as criminality is erected as an altar upon which the repressed classes are ritualistically sacrificed. But the dominant class does not engage in this ritual with a bald-faced, cynical consciousness. For to do so would provoke even in that class, self-righteous feelings of self-condemnation and fear of justifiable punishment. In order to escape flagellation by its own bad conscience and escape the need to atone for its repression and dispossession of its repressed subordinate classes, the egocentric ruling class must, through defensive self-deception and distorting lies, deny its culpability and responsibility for sacrificing for its own self aggrandizement, those same subordinate classes or groups.

Personality and Culture

Like personality, society or culture can be said to possess a modal character or identity, and correlated behavioral orientation. Society may also be said to possess a collective consciousness, self-image and world-view. A society may be usefully schematized as consisting of any number of dynamically interacting socioeconomic group complexes, class or social status divisions. A society's effect on its environment — its behavioral style (standing and prestige), its self-image, degree of internal integration, harmony, equilibrium, and integrity — are functions of the dynamic nature and character of its constituent intergroup relations, its geophysical, historical, cultural and other circumstances. In sum, the modal character of a society may be said to be a manifestation of the interactive outcome of its intergroup complexes and of its interactive relations with external sources. The nature and character of the interactions between its constituent groups or classes determine to a measurable extent the nature of its "social symptoms" such as criminality.

Applying somewhat simplistically the psychoanalytic model of personality to social processes, we contend that societies may be usefully perceived as possessing societal group or class ego complexes, and that these group complexes interact dynamically. A society's ruling and/or influential groups, which may be construed to represent its social and societal ego complex along with their collective perceptions and behavioral styles, dominate what may be called the societal personality. That is, society may be perceived as possessing a central group ego complex comprised of its dominant and most influential group(s) among other group complexes with which it (or they) influentially interacts. The central societal ego group complex evinces a collective consciousness, self-consciousness, and self-image which it seeks to present as the exclusive and legitimate projections of the societal personality. The central societal ego group complex, like the individual ego complex, is motivated by self-preservation, defensive security, desire for social status, power, hegemony, material comforts and pleasures. Generally, the central group societal complex seeks to regulate and maintain its interactions with the other group complexes so as to derive the greatest quantity and the highest quality of benefits for itself. Social symptoms such as criminality, its type and distribution, may reflect the outcome of the central group complex's attempts to gain and/or maintain socioeconomic advantages over the other social groups which are deprived of such advantages.

To reiterate, the societal central complex may be roughly identified as the society's ruling/managing classes and other influential groups. In the United States of America, the central societal ego complex is represented by the White American ruling and middle classes and related White groups. These classes and groups generally seek to determine and govern the character and behavior of the societal whole in such ways as to maintain and enhance their wealth, power, and dominance. The activities, resources, powers, and perceptions of the subordinate group complex and less influential social groups, are regulated and exploited by the White American community in ways that legitimize and strengthen that ruling complex's dominant position. The subordinate group ego complex refers to the African American community and related low-status groups. As far as the White American community is concerned, the African American community and related groups function to support and service its dominance. The White community legislates, enforces, and reinforces, the role-functions and behavioral boundaries of the African American community in accordance with its dominance needs. By these means the place of the African American community, relative to the White American community, is "legitimized."[Consequently, autonomous displacement by the African American community, labeled illegitimate or illegal by the White American community, may be perceived by that community as threatening its well-being and synonymously the well-being of the societal whole. The well-being of the societal whole, of course, is closely identified with the "well-being" of the White American community.

As long as African Americans perform according to the roles prescribed for them by the White American community ego complex; as long as they maintain their defined places, and form the background against which the preferred White American complex is projected; as long as they reasonably fit the self-serving stereotypes imposed on them by the White American complex, the African American community attains a functional invisibility, a shadowy existence at the periphery of the consciousness of the White community.

In its peripheral, functional invisibility, the African American community contributes to the character, power, and self-concept of the dominant White American community. However, when and if the African American community threatens to move or actually moves beyond its functional invisibility; when it attempts to escape its role definition, acts on its own volition and thereby escapes dominant group controls; when it challenges the legitimacy and relative autonomy of the White American community, that community responds repressively. The repressive responses of the dominant White community complex to the autonomous activities of the African American community complex, interact dynamically to create societal symptoms, some of which may be labeled criminal.]

As a result of White American communal repression and projective stereotyping of the African American community, some segments of the African American community may actually assume a malevolent, anti-societal, self-destructive character. In this instance, the dominant White community complex in effect produces illnesses, symptoms, ailments and complaints in the body politic of American society through its egoistical repression of the African American community, and utilizes those ailments to further its psychological and dominance needs. Thus, it reaps both primary and secondary benefits from its own created illnesses.

However, in order to reduce any guilt which may result from consciously acknowledging responsibility for inflicting pain on the African American communities and exploiting that affliction; to escape self-condemnation for violating its own vaunted morals, standards, principles and projected self-image, the dominant White American community must deny and distort its own role in producing the resultant symptoms. It accomplishes this by a number of means, including authoritatively declaring that the symptoms are the result of the inherent nature of African American, and by developing a studied inattention to or disregard of its instigative responsibility for producing those symptoms. By these means the White American community can deny that it is itself deluded, maladjusted, abnormal...perhaps psychotic, and therefore not in need of curative restructuring.

Dominant and Subordinate Societal
Class Complexes in America

The modal societal character or personality of the United States of America is dominated by what may be called the collective White American ego complex. This societal conglomerate of Caucasians, or more commonly, "White people," is composed mainly of the descendants of western European Protestants who form its nuclear component and of other lesser-esteemed European ethnic group subcomplexes. The rest of the American societal personality is composed of subordinate societal "minority" group complexes, (e.g., Asians, Latinos, "Blacks," Africans) and a plethora of minor ethnic and religious groups. These subordinate ethnically-based societal group complexes differ in their national social and economic standing, power and prestige. While the subordinate societal group complexes interact mutually and interdependently with widely varying degrees of intensity, they all move within the gravitational field force and pull of the dominant White American group complex. It is this European eurocentrically based complex, particularly its White Anglo-Saxon Protestant core component, which seeks to control the behavior of its "minority" subordinate group complexes in ways consonant with its socioeconomic, politico-cultural, psychophysical goals and programs.

The White American group complex seeks to project its collective will, consciousness, self-image, values, ideals, etc., as legitimately representative of the whole societal personality. The White American group complex projects its face as the persona of the sociopolitical whole. It seeks, through the use of various psychosocial mechanisms (e.g., denial, deception, distortion and repression) to impose its mental and material hegemony on the subordinate group complexes in ways compatible with its perceived needs for power and regulatory dominance of the national and international body politic. It seeks to project as supreme and ideal its vaunted self-image and identity, to represent its collective consciousness as the only legitimate and "God-given" reality, and to regulate and arrogate to itself the bulk of the wealth, resources, and energy of the nation and globe in ways consonant to its national and international appetite and advantage. This can only be accomplished by instigation of repressively regulatory, hegemonic interactions with its subordinate group complexes, particularly the African-based group complex which potentially represents its most challenging rival for power and control. In order to satisfy its paranoid need to develop and defend its power and hegemony, which was and is based on its brutal and murderous repression and exploitation especially of indigenous American and African groups complexes, coupled with its need to deny the breaking of its own vaunted moral and constitutional ideals, the dominant White American ego complex must through various defensive rationalizations and other self-deceptive schemes repress the ugly realities of its ghastly deeds.

White Domination, Black Criminality

The perpetual domination of African Americans by White Americans psychically requires the White American criminalization of the African male, i.e., the White American perception of the African male as inherently criminal. In the context of White American domination there is no innocent Black male, just Black male criminals who have not yet been detected, apprehended or convicted. Their mere presence inspires in White Americans, fears of being assaulted, raped, robbed, or some other indefinable dread of being criminally victimized. Fantasies of the sexual molestation of White females by rapacious Black males are common to the White American male and female consciousness, and are frequent themes of their literary, cinematic, and pornographic productions.

For a very large percentage of White Americans, young Black males, sexual promiscuity, and criminality are synonymous. In the dominant White American consciousness the African male is existentially guilty, (i.e., he is guilty by his mere existence) for merely having the audacity of being alive. There is a pervasive feeling among many White Americans that their world would be much more secure if all young Black males were imprisoned, solitarily confined to their ghettos, or kept under constant surveillance. It is no quirky coincidence that such perceptions, feelings and attitudes toward African American males occur most prevalently within the context of White American dominance. Ultimately, criminality of the Black male regardless of its nature, truth or reality, resides in any act or attitude on the part of Black males which appears to White Americans to defy White American authority, control or dominance. It is White America which defines criminality and writes the criminal justice codes. It writes these codes not in the interest of justice as defined by its own moral code, but in the interest of maintaining, justifying and enforcing its continued dominance of the African American community.

In the interest of maintaining and justifying continuity of the White American community, the African male is not only readily suspected of committing crimes, but is actively provoked and seduced into criminality by his White American accusers and persecutors. White America's need to dominate Black America creates the need to perceive the African male as criminal, and to actualize African male criminality by socializing or ritualizing him into it by dent of judicial witchcraft. Such maneuvers are necessary in order to justify the White American community's repression of African Americans and psychodynamically defend the collective White American ego complex. The need to projectively perceive the African male as criminal, to psychosocially and politicoeconomically condition his criminality, is reflective of repressed White American guilt and criminality. The White American community must realize, though it will not admit it, that crimes committed in the service of White American domination — the rape and robbery of nations, the murder and exploitation of native peoples and their lands, the denial of the humanity of non-European peoples, the enslavement, lynching, racial discrimination against and disenfranchisement of African Americans — infinitely outweigh the alleged crimes of African American men. White American and European denial of their historical criminal subjugation and vicious exploitation of African peoples and their ongoing defense of their continuing criminal subordination of African peoples have psychically infected the African mind with a variant of White American/European communal psychopathology. Such Eurocentric psychopathology is manifested in *Black-on-Black* crime, the subject of this essay.

Black male criminality is the stepchild of White male criminality. The White male, in order to enhance and protect his self-image, enjoy the material wealth, power, and political advantages of his criminality, must deny truth and reality: he must not experience the guilty conscience which would result from an acknowledgment and acceptance of his own criminality and psychopathy. His malevolent incrustations must be smoothed over and his criminal dross transmuted to gold. The collective White American ego complex must deny and distort reality if it is to persist in perceiving itself as God's *chosen*; as sanctified in face of its beastification of the African Americans (particularly males) and its thingification of others.

QUANTIFYING A MYTH:

STATISTICS AND BLACK CRIMINALITY

THE CITY SUN, *July 18-24, 1990*
Within five years after the Civil War, the Black percentage of the prison population went from close to zero percent to 33 percent.

Then, as now, the Black prison population performed an economic and political function for the benefit of Whites.

— CLINTON COX
Racism: The Hole In America's Heart

Eurocentric Criminology

CRIME AND CRIMINAL behavior regardless of temporal or cultural definition, occur not in a vacuum, but within a complex matrix of interpersonal, social, intergroup relations, and other eco-psychological forces. Crime and criminality, their existential vicissitudes, and emblematic meanings, can only be usefully and appropriately deciphered and pragmatically dealt with within the context of these forces. Crime and criminality are social phenomena and are reflective of the social system within which they occur. To discuss crime and criminality without reference to a social system is to engage in meaningless discussion. Yet this approach to the study of criminality is typical of much of academic criminological and behavioral science theoretical writings. Academic emphasis on intrapsychic and personality factors at the expense of extensive consideration of the more important socioeconomic, sociopolitical factors as sources of criminal behavior, makes academic criminologists in effect apologists and rationalizers for the White American-dominated politico-economic status quo. It must be recognized that both the intrapsychic and the personal are social products, and are creatively reflective of their sociopolitical, socioecological experiential and environmental background. The idea of personality as relatively isolated and unreflective of its social interactive history and environment, as motivated by purely internal motives, is an illusion. Moreover, such a concept is a dangerous myth and a psychological conspiracy perpetrated by the ruling groups in society to escape their responsibility for producing and perpetuating negative social forces which produce antisocial individuals and groups.

The disciplines of criminology, the behavioral and social sciences, like all the other institutional disciplines in a racist/ class society, seek to rationalize and present an apologia for the political status quo without losing respectability. To accomplish this they must, in effect, promote the decontextualization of crime and criminality. That is, they tend to divorce crime and criminality from their socioecological and psychohistorical contexts and present them as small-group, subcultural, and personality problems. Standard explanations and approaches take crime out of the total context which sires it, out of the politico-economic context which gives it shape and form, and places it within the context of a mythical quasi-innate "criminal" personality, class, subculture, or group. How one can have an innately criminal personality or be a member of a quasi-innately criminal or subcultural group when what is deemed criminal changes over time and place? Therefore the definition of what may be called criminal today was not called so yesterday nor will it be called such tomorrow, is rarely pragmatically and realistically dealt with. This is also the case with reference to which group defines what is deemed or not deemed criminal. How the ruling groups define and apply the criminal code and how such definition and application by the ruling class may instigate "criminality" in segments of its subject population and inject a "criminal" implant in some of its constituent "personalities" as well, is very rarely discussed or examined by establishment criminologists.

At its liberal best, establishment criminology, as intimated by Tony Platt in his article, *Prospects for a Radical Criminology in the United States*, is reformist, i.e., "[it believes] that it is possible to create a well-regulated, stable and humanitarian system of criminal justice under the present economic and political arrangements." He goes on to say that "establishment criminologists...reform proposals are invariably formulated within the framework of corporate capitalism and are designed to shape new adjustments to existing political and economic conditions."

We might add at this juncture that establishment reform proposals are formulated and practically designed to shape African peoples' adjustments to existing and ongoing Eurocentric political and economic conditions — and more fundamentally, to the conditions of White over Black, to the conditions of White supremacy. Platt further proposed that Eurocentric establishment reformism:

> has helped to create probation and parole, the juvenile court system, reformatories and half-way houses, the indeterminate sentence, adjustment and diagnostic centers, public defenders, youth service bureaus and other "reforms" which have served to strengthen the power of the state over the poor, Third World communities and youth. As the American Friend Services Committee has observed, "the legacy of a century of reform effort is an increasingly repressive penal system and over-crowded courts dispensing assembly-line justice.[7]

The above quotation implies that reform or charity under the aegis of the dominant White ruling class, of white supremacy, serves to maintain such dominance and supremacy. Reform is what reform does. If the institution of reform measures do not help to liberate the oppressed, and furthermore, actually worsens

---

[7] *American Friends Service Committee, 1979:9.*

their oppression, then such measures functionally serve the power status quo. Criminal reformism which does not make its objective the eradication of the crimogenic politicoeconomic system is designed to put a "benign" face on racist, ruling class oppression; to make oppression palliative to the oppressed.

Parenti observes:

> ...the United states locks up more people per capita, for longer times, than any other advanced industrial nation except South Africa. By 1985, there were more than twice as many Americans in prison than in 1970 and the numbers of police more than doubled between 1957 and 1977, yet during this period crime rates increased over 400 percent. Nor are the more punitive states, like Texas, safer than others.[8]

The major problem which plagues establishment criminology, conservative, liberal, or otherwise, is that it is written and promulgated from the "top down," (i.e., written and practiced by an academic elite, criminological technocrats, namely consultants, judges, wardens and others who have a vested interest in the regulation of crime and criminal activity). These persons are employed by the crimogenic system which is the very source of much of the crime and criminality they write about, and work at controlling. Consequently, their professional practice can be only ameliorative at best. The logical solution to the problem they propose to resolve never includes the eradication of its source, the crimogenic system itself. Causal explanations which include the character, perspectives, and behavior of the ruling group as a part of the problem, are designated "radical" by establishment academicians and thereby rendered null and void. When crime continues unabated in a society or community, that society or community is crimogenic. In gist, it gives birth to criminality by virtue of its structural characteristics as determined by any number of currently active historical, intergroup, and/or other internal and external factors.

---

[8] Parenti, M. *Democracy for the Few*. 5th ed. New York: St. Martin Press, 1987.

Consequently, year after year, from the halls of academia, police desks and judges' chambers, we are presented with tired causal explanations of the factors which allegedly underlie criminal behavior — poverty, under-employment, broken homes, drugs, poor education, rising expectations, the age of anxiety, anomie, malaise, personality, ethnicity, community instability, brain biochemistry and so on. But these explanations never satisfy. And the Black American community continues to see its collective life ooze away in a genocidal pool of blood. The case may be that these explanations, while not completely irrelevant and untrue, while providing some enlightenment and footing for the practical amelioration of crime and criminality in the African American community, may be but manifestations of a deeper, more profound set of variables.

Crime in the Black Community

It is now time for the African American community to provide solutions to the criminal problems which beset it and which threaten its very survival. Criminality in the African American community is not merely the subject matter for theoretical debates nor merely the stuff of scholarly treatises. It's a matter of life and death. The following statistics taken from the National Urban League's *The State Of Black America 1988*, indicate the serious nature and urgency of "Black-on-Black" crime:

Arrests
In 1986, blacks comprised approximately 12 percent of the United States population. Yet, during that year blacks accounted for...46.5 percent of all arrests for violent crimes... Of the persons arrested for murder in 1986, blacks accounted for 48 percent of the total. That same year, blacks accounted for 46.6 percent of all arrests for rape, 62 percent of all arrests for robbery, 39.8 percent for assault, 29.5 percent for burglary, 30.1 percent for theft, and 34.7 percent for auto theft.

...In respect to city arrests, blacks accounted for 30.8 percent of the total arrests made in 1986. Of the number of city arrests made for violent crimes (murder, forcible rape, robbery, and aggravated assault) that year, blacks accounted for almost half (49.5 percent), 34.3 percent for property offenses (burglary, larceny, theft, motor theft, and arson).

With respect to persons under 18 years of age who were arrested, blacks made up 25.1 percent of the total arrests made in 1986. In addition, blacks accounted for 54.9 percent of those under 18 who were arrested for violent crimes, 27.1 percent for property offenses, and 30.3 percent of all index crimes during 1986.

Incarceration

The number of blacks in prisons, as compared to the number of blacks in the population, is a second method of assessing crime and its relationship to Afro-Americans. The latest prisoner survey, which was conducted on December 31, 1984, showed that there was a total of 462,422 prisoners in state and federal institutions. Of that number, 209,673, or 45 percent, were black. With respect to federal institutions, 10,786 out of total population of 34,263 were black, constituting 31 percent. Out of the 428,179 in state institutions, 198,887 or 46 percent were black. As of June 30, 1984, 40 percent of all jail inmates throughout the nation were black. A similar situation exists for black youth. On February 1, 1985, 18,269, 61 percent of a total of 29,969 juveniles held in public facilities were black.

On March 1, 1987, there was a total of 1,874 prisoners under sentence of death. Of that number, 777 or 42 percent were black.

Victimization

...surveys reveal the following:

While Whites are more vulnerable to personal theft, blacks are more vulnerable than Whites to violent crime.

A higher percentage of black households than White or other minority households are touched by crime.

Blacks have the highest victimization rates for rape, robbery, and assault.

Blacks are more likely to be victims of violent crime than Whites or members of other racial groups.

Young black males have the highest violent crime rates.

Based on the number of vehicles owned, black heads of households were victims of motor vehicle theft at a higher rate than Whites or members of other minority groups.

Most violent crimes against blacks were committed by black offenders (84 percent). Black on Black Crime Decide and longer

Of all black households in 1985, 27 percent had been touched by crime. Two years later, black households continue to be more vulnerable than Whites for violent crime (5.4 percent vs. 4.6 percent), burglary (7.6 percent vs. 5 percent), and theft in and around the home (9.1 percent vs. 7.9 percent).

The chances of a person, black or white, being the victim of crime is directly related to family income: The lower the income, the greater the chances of victimization. As for specific types of crime, the typical American has a 1-in-133 chance of being murdered. However, for black males the chances are 1 in 21.

The leading cause of death among black males between the ages of 15 and 24 years of age is homicide. Approximately 42 per 100,000 blacks between the ages of 15-24 die from homicide. This compares with about eight per 100,000 Whites in the same age group. For nearly all age groups, however, homicide victimization rates do not differ significantly even though there are considerably fewer blacks than Whites nationwide.

...the problem of crime in the black community is complicated by many other problems. Currently, one of the most severe of those other problems is drugs.

The Drug Problem
...blacks are disproportionately represented among person's estimated to be abusers of alcohol or drugs relative to their numbers in the U.S. population.

A note of caution is in order in regard to the statistics just cited. William Ryan, in his book, *Blaming The Victim*, indicates why this must be the case:

...the FBI Crime Report — with all its tables and charts, its fatuously precise summations (1,605,700 burglaries, indeed) — is one of the most preposterously non-factual documents ever to roll off the print presses of the U.S. Government Printing

Office. As a basis for serious discussion of social problems and social policies, it is approximately as useful as Madame Zelda's Lucky Number Dream Book.

Ryan further intimated that regardless of race, crime is endemic to the United States. America is a country whose population is circumscribed and immersed in crime. The FBI's Crime Index rate grossly underestimates the overall crime rate. The actual crime rate may be at least two or three times the rate reported by the FBI. He reports evidence which suggests that the greater portion of crime in the U.S. is "hidden."

Stephan Chorover, after studying what he refers to as the "false assumption that incarceration is a valid index of criminality," concluded that:

> ...*criminal acts are far more equitably distributed across society than are the acts of punishment.* Of the crimes punishable by imprisonment, 98.5 percent go unpunished. The 1.5 percent who are prisoners should not be confused with the total population of criminal offenders. When the Ratzenbach Commission examined the prison population the picture that emerged pointed overwhelmingly to the background features that are socioeconomic. It was found that the most consistently observed antecedents of incarceration are poverty, lack of schooling, joblessness, and family instability.[9] (Emphasis added)

So-called white-collar crime is ordinarily not even counted as crime even though its perpetrators are specifically known to criminal justice officials. Though corporate crime, which robs Americans of billions of dollars endangers the health and destroys the lives of millions of Americans and non-Americans, such activities are not often perceived as crime. While Whites commit the majority of crime in America, crime, particularly "crime in the streets," is seen as an African American monopoly. Ryan very pointedly reports that "out of the total spectrum of crime, very little is committed in the streets." The hue and cry in America for "law and order" is essentially a White American-coded plea for containment of alleged Black criminality — and

---

[9] Chorover, Stephan. *From Genesis to Genocide: The Meaning of Human Nature and the Power of Behavior Control.* Cambridge, Mass.: MIT Press, 1980.

ultimately a plea for the containment of the African American community.

> The trouble with the official crime picture is that it has the effect of grossly distorting the average citizen's image of what crime is all about. It minimizes and deflects attention from one kind of crime (the common kind that one's neighbors commit) and exaggerates and spotlights another, less common, kind (the code name is "crime-in-the-street" which is presumably committed by "criminals").[10]

Ryan asks:

> Why does the American public respond so strongly to the issue of law and order?
> There are at least two reasons. One is that the myopic view represented in the conventional wisdom about crime seems to provide at least some vague rationale for the tasks we set for our police; and it is comforting to keep the illusion that police are engaged in law enforcement. Another is that it permits us to keep believing that crime is fertilized by the slums and nurtured by low-socioeconomic status. We can then go on talking about some mythical separate group of criminals — most of whom, of course, are poor or black or both, — as dangerous and threatening to the life of the community. *We do this through the device of defining as criminal only persons arrested by the police* (Emphasis added).
>
> * * * *
>
> *...a set of studies show that there is no substantial relationship between social class and the commission of crimes, but there is a very marked relationship between class and conviction for crime* (Emphasis added). The lesson of all this is plain: the fact that half or more of the persons arrested for crimes of personal violence, and that forty to fifty per cent of all prisoners in jails and penitentiaries are black says nothing at all about the criminality of black people. And that an even higher proportion of persons arrested are poor and imprisoned sheds no light whatever on the criminality of the poor. These facts only identify the objects of police and court activity. There are law

---

[10] Ryan, W. *Blaming the Victim*. New York: Random House, 1971.

violators and there are law violators; one kind gets arrested, the other kind is usually left alone.

* * * *

...the major determinant of police action is not so much the commission of a crime as the identity of the supposed criminal.

* * * *

We must judge why we hire the policemen by the evidence. Presumably we hire them to do what they, in fact do: arrest Black people and poor people. In functional terms, it would be hard to evade the conclusion that the major task we give to our police is to control potentially disruptive or troublesome groups in the population.

* * * *

Ryan further intimates that White America's perception of "crime" as a "Black thing" and that the control or psychopolitical, socioeconomic ostracism of the Black community is based on the belief that crime is far more prevalent in that community than in the White community. This belief is further supported by the oft-projected belief that the criminality of the poor (*read*: Black) reflects the warping of their character and behavior by the negative social conditions under which they live (i.e., it is not acknowledged that the social conditions under which they live are created and maintained by White America and if the character of a segment of the Black community is criminalized by its living conditions, then White America must ultimately accept its responsibility for creating "Black crime"). Related beliefs include the generally accepted ideas that lower class criminals (*read*: "Black") form a distinct subculture in the general population and that the overriding purpose of the police is to "quarantine" this subgroup in order to control and suppress its criminal activity.

This set of [beliefs] is an extremely plausible and acceptable version of Blaming the Victim, perhaps the most plausible of all formulations I have discussed. *It is the most outrageous collection of non-facts [unsubstantiated beliefs] imaginable.** But the speciousness of the argumentation is not easy to detect. It is difficult, in the first place, to think of the person we call a criminal as a victim at all. In what way is the mugger, the purse-snatcher, the thug who beats up our neighbor in Central

Park, a victim? How can the processes of criminal justice, in any sense, be defined as Blaming the Victim?

* * * *

The real truth is that arrest, trial and punishment of persons accused of breaking the law is very tenuously related to the enforcement of law and the deterrence of crime, and has only a remote relationship with any abstract entity as justice* (*Emphasis added). As J. Edgar Hoover once said in a moment of perhaps unintentional candor, *"justice is incidental to law and order."*[11]

Criminality, both alleged and actual, in the African American community indicts White American-dominated society and culture. However, while those who dominate this society and culture are quick to take credit and responsibility for their exaggerated positive characteristics and productivity, they are loathe to take credit and responsibility for one of its outstanding negative characteristics — the oppressive criminalization of the African American community.

Every respectable, half-way competent social scientist who has paid attention at all to the issues of crime and delinquency knows: that crime is endemic in all social classes: that the administration of justice is grossly biased against the Negro and the lower class defendant; *that arrest and imprisonment is a process reserved almost exclusively for the black and the poor; and that the major function of the police is the preservation, not only of the public order, but of the social order — that is, of inequality between man and man.* To blather on and on about the slum as a "breeding place of crime," about lower class culture as a generating milieu of delinquency" — a presumably liberal explanation of the prevalence of crime among the poor — is to engage (surely, almost consciously) in ideological warfare against the poor in the interest of maintaining the status quo. It is one of the most detestable forms of Blaming the Victim.[12] (Emphasis added)

---

[11] Ibid.

[12] Ibid.

Parenti corroborates this conclusion in citing the following facts among others:

Leniency is for the affluent, severity for the indigent. Only 18 percent of white-collar embezzlers go to prison for an average of fifteen months and many have their sentences dropped. But 89 percent of working poor people convicted of larceny spend an average of ten-and-a-half years behind bars. Some examples might serve: a judge imposed a small fine on a stockbroker who had made $20 million through illegal stock manipulation and, on the same day, sentenced an unemployed Black man to one year in jail for stealing a television set from a truck shipment.

* * * *

Blacks tend to get substantially longer prison terms than whites convicted of the same crimes, even when the Black person is a first time offender and the White person a second- or third-time offender.

* * * *

To sum up: poor and working-class persons, the uneducated, and the racial minorities are more likely to be arrested, less likely to be released on bail, more likely to be induced to plead guilty, more likely to go without a pretrial hearing even though entitled to one, less likely to have a jury trial if tried, more likely to be convicted and receive a harsh sentence, and less likely to receive probation or a suspended sentence than are mobsters, business-people, and upper- and middle-class Whites in general.[13]

Clinton Cox in a review of American criminal justice practices noted that:

...Blacks serve more time in jail than whites for the same offenses: murder, 91.7 months for Blacks versus 79.8 months for whites; rape, 55 months for Blacks versus 43.9 for whites; kidnapping, 41 months for Blacks to 37 for whites; and robbery 37.4 for Blacks to 33.3 for whites.[14]

---

[13] Parenti, M. *Democracy for the Few*. 5th ed. New York: St. Martin Press, 1987.

[14] Cox, C. *Racism: The Hole in America's Heart*, THE CITY SUN, July 18-24, 1990.

Thus, arrest records, prison statistics and the like, are more a reflection of the social status of the alleged criminal than of the nature of criminality across all class lines. The war against crime may be more accurately depicted as a war of the privileged against the underprivileged, of the advantaged against the disadvantaged. Arrest records and related statistics poignantly point out the class bias of the American criminal justice practices. The foregoing discussion was not designed to deny the reality and scale of crime in the African American community. Crime and criminality there are very real and much too prevalent. The discussion was designed to emphasize the fact that crime is not exclusively endemic to the Black community and to point out the way in which criminal justice practices and crime statistics are used to create the false and scandalous impression that African Americans have some sort of monopoly on crime and are "inherently" more criminal than are White Americans. The intriguing issue raised by the discussion just presented is: What purposes do the racist police and criminal justice practices, as well as the biased presentation of crime statistics, serve within the context of White-dominated American society?

The Myth of Black Violence: A Critique

A general conclusion which can be drawn from the foregoing discussion is that FBI crime reports, arrest, imprisonment, and other criminal justice statistics are more often than not used to quantify the common social belief that Blacks are inherently more criminal or violence-prone than are Whites. Moreover, such statistics are used to justify the racial status quo and to institute more legal and illegal measures against the human and civil rights of African Americans. As cited above, both William Ryan and Michael Parenti argue persuasively that crime statistics as generally presented are more reflective of race and class bias in law enforcement than of the reality of crime in America. In an op-ed column entitled *The Myth of Black Violence*, written by Evan Stark and published in *The New York Times*, July 18, 1990, evidence was presented to refute the precept that Black youth are more "violence-prone" than are White youth.

Citing statistics from FBI crime reports Stark tentatively surmised that:

...homicide is the major cause of death for younger black males, as well as for black women under 40.

Inner city blacks appear to be particularly violence-prone. The homicide rate for young black males living in standard metropolitan areas is twice that for young blacks living in other locations.

The figures on black teen-agers seem more ominous still. From 1977 to 1982, more than half of the juvenile arrests for the most violent crimes were among black teen-agers, and the relative rate of incarceration for black as against white youth was an astounding 44 to 1.

However, in accord with the arguments made by Ryan and Parenti — that data of the kind just cited is more indicative of police (as well as average White American) attitudes and behavior than of racial differences — Stark states that:

This alternative view is supported by national surveys of crime victims, a far more accurate source of information about crimes committed than arrest reports. According to the FBI, for example, the proportion of blacks arrested for aggravated assault in 1987 was more than three times greater than the proportion of whites. But the National Crime Survey, based on victim interviews, found that the actual proportion of blacks and whites committing aggravated assault in 1987 was virtually identical: 32 per 1,000 for blacks; 31 per 1,000 for whites.

Similarly, The National Youth Survey involved 1,725 youths 11 to 17 years of age, whose law-violating behavior between 1976 and 1980 was determined by confidential interviews. The survey reported that, with the exception of 1976, "no significant race differences were found in any of the violent or serious offense scales."

Based on the evidence he presents Stark concludes that Black youth is no more "violence-prone" than is White youth and that "race does not determine who initiates violence." However, Stark notes the disturbing fact that "fatal outcomes are far more likely when blacks are involved [in violence]." Despite the comparatively more fatal outcome of Black-on-Black violence, Stark argues that the question "...is not why blacks are more violent than whites — they may not be — but why are the consequences of

violent confrontations for blacks so much more severe?" Stark
suggests the following answer:

> The belief that blacks are more "violence prone" leads to a
> double standard in police response. When white and black teen-
> agers commit the same offense, police are seven times more
> likely to charge black teen-agers with a felony, and courts are
> more likely to imprison the teen-ager.
>
> But the belief that violence among inner-city blacks is
> normal also leads police and courts to tolerate levels of violence
> among black adults that would not be accepted from other
> groups, particularly in and around the home. The result is that
> arrest and imprisonment are deemed appropriate only after
> the violence escalates.
>
> This pattern is illustrated most dramatically with domestic
> violence — a major cause of death among black women under
> 40. The typical domestic homicide is preceded by assaults; law
> enforcement fails to intervene until a serious injury of fatality
> occurs. Homicides among black males, including gang offenses,
> often have a similar history.

While we will not challenge the validity of Stark's explanation of the relatively more fatal outcome of Black-on-Black
violence, we do challenge its depth, completeness, and utility.
In his attempt to demonstrate that Black youths are no more
violence-prone than are White youths, and his avoidance of the
question as to whether Blacks are more violent than Whites,
Stark preempts himself from undertaking a most intriguing and
informative exploration into the social psychology and psychodynamics of Black-on-Black violence.

To demonstrate that two persons or groups possess to an
equal degree a particular characteristic, trait or tendency, does
not necessarily imply that they will express such a characteristic,
trait, or tendency to an equal degree, in the same way, with the
same intensity, or with the same outcome. Equal drives under
different conditions can bring about unequal results. It is indeed
quite possible that Blacks are *less* "violence-prone" than Whites
yet due to any number of factors which may tend to intensify
their violence-proneness they may, under certain circumstances,
express themselves more violently than Whites who live under
different circumstances. Under current conditions, to compare

Black and White violence-proneness, particularly on a one-to-one basis, is to compare apples and oranges. To make historical and contemporaneous White-on-White or White-on-Black violence in quality and quantity comparable to Black-on-White and Black-on-Black violence, is to add insult to injury to the history and character of Black peoples.

We must not too hastily conclude that all violent behavior is motivated by "violence-proneness" or "criminal drives." It is arguably possible that many, if not most, violent attacks are rooted in socially acquired, socially approved "drives" and incentives — "good" drives and incentives whose satisfaction and acquisition have been, more often than not, frustrated, twisted and distorted by the same society which created them. "The road to Hell is paved with good intentions."

African American and liberal scholars must resist the seductive temptation to preemptively prove every difference between Blacks and Whites, particularly apparently negative ones, a myth, implying that certain differences do not really exist. This tendency among African Americans to accept the most direly *negative* situations if it can be demonstrated that White Americans are suffering to the same degree, is unhealthy and counterproductive. To be the same is not necessarily to be equal. The fact that many African Americans strive mightily to prove themselves to be "the same as," therefore "equal to" the Whites who enslaved and colonized them; who physically and psychologically abuse, economically and socially exploit them, is indicative of just how maladjusted the African psyche has become under the brutality of European oppression. The only hope for the world is that Africans and other peoples, including Europeans, make themselves as positively different from the past and current European proclivities and other oppressive peoples as is humanely possible.

To demonstrate that a belief, e.g., Blacks are more violent than Whites, is a myth does not dispose of the need to explain why the myth exists in the first place and what are its social, socioeconomic and psychopolitical functions. Because a myth may be just that, untrue, a lie, does not mean that its psychological and social effects are unreal or illusory.

The myth of Black violence serves important functions in American society and in the world — those of justifying and rationalizing White supremacy. It also functions to organize the consciousness, inter-, intra-group and interpersonal relations among Black peoples, their relations to White peoples, such that through their behavior Black people will continue to empower their oppressors by engaging in self-oppression.

Nevertheless, when all is said and done it must be admitted, as it was by Stark, that "...the myth of black violence nonetheless has real and tragic consequences." These consequences must be undone, remedied and prevented. However the statistics may be presented, the prevalence of Black-on-Black violent criminality is a reality which must be acknowledged and neutralized by the African American community. This requires a thorough understanding of its causes and the reorganization of the community based on that understanding if the viability of African peoples around the world is to be secured and protected.

Stark is correct when he implies that Black violence is to a significant extent the product of racism [*read*: White supremacy] and that "What needs to be changed is racism ..." [*read*: What needs to be eradicated is White supremacy]. But he is not correct when he asserts that Black manhood need not be changed. We believe that the very necessary and sufficient catalyst for the changing and eradication of White racism/White supremacy is the prior transformation of Black manhood.

The Crucible of Identity

[The construction and organization of group and personal identity are of the utmost importance to individual, group functionality and survival. All groups or cultures, if they are to survive, autonomously exist and prosper, see the establishment of the identity of themselves and their constituents as their major role. This is accomplished through their controlling the nature their environment, social experience, information, social interaction and symbols. Cultural symbols are utilized to help construct, maintain, and regulate the identity and behavior of the constituents of a cultural group in such ways as to advance their individual group and cultural interests and successfully defend themselves against those who would exploit, dominate, abuse or destroy them.] All human societies act on the basis of some kind of shared identity, sense of commonality or shared fate. When the identity of the individual or group is manipulated by an alien entity, then that manipulated individual's or group's viability rests in hands other than its own. That individual's and/or the group's lot in life then moves beyond his or its self-control.

Anytime an alienated individual's or group's self-restriction — self-alienation, self-abnegation, and self-destruction — is required to meet the needs of those who control and define his or its identity, then that individual or group tends to feel compelled, pushed by fate, to engage in self-alienating, self-abnegating, self-destructive behaviors. The conditions of subordination, *third-world-ism*, blatant exploitation, all-round vulnerability to destruction, self-destructiveness, and Black-on-Black criminality which plague African peoples, are the result of the fact that these peoples have for too long permitted their identity, and therefore their destiny, to be determined by Europeans. European intuition and political science realize that personal and group identity represent organized systems of needs, motives, desires, assumptions, presumptions, feelings, competencies, and knowledges. These correlated and interdependent factors together mediate, maintain and regulate interactive relationships with the individual's or group's biological, material, and social environment. The identity complex, which is essentially sociohistorical in its inception, construction and function, is the nodal and focal reference point for translating and processing experience, thereby shaping consciousness, and through the shaping of consciousness the shaping of experience and behavior. African Americans, and Africans in general, have permitted the sociohistorical processes crucial to the construction of their identity to be controlled by Europeans and White Americans. In doing this they have ceded their self-control and self-determination to Europeans. This lack of self-control and self-determination, and the resultant reactionary relationship they have to the world as well as to their own feelings, are the central causative factors in the maladaptiveness of the collective and individual African personality. Any rehabilitation program involving Africans and African Americans must make the reclamation of the inherent right of Africans to construct themselves after their own images, and the reconstruction of their identity, preeminent therapeutic goals.

The Black-on-Black criminal must be made to realize that one of his principal problems is one of *identity*. He must understand how the criminal complex with which he currently identifies was constructed by Europeans for their own benefit and his ultimate demise. His criminal identity must be exorcized and a new, authentic one constructed through a new infusion of Afrocentric information, supportive social interactions, the development of new competencies, knowledges and associations. He must come to understand that what he perceives as "his" needs, desires, ideals, motives, goals, etc., are manufactured and implanted in him by Europeans for the benefit of Europeans at the price of the destruction of his humanity, body, community, and future. He must understand that his vain attempts to satisfy those introjected desires, etc., do not represent what it means to be free, to be a man, to have arrived at the pinnacle of human possibilities, or success, but instead represent the grossest form of slavery, animality, and thinginess. He must understand that Europeans and their so-called civilizations, the human behaviors, attitudes, and relations they engender, represent the most destructive factors existent in the universe today and to identify with them is to identify with a self-destructive spirit within himself, a spirit which makes his own existence pointless and meaningless. He must understand that he can only achieve authentic honor, fulfillment, love, respect, security, belonging-ness, distinction, through self and group empowerment. He can gain transcendence only through the full acceptance of his African identity, the reclamation of his birthrights, through economic and cultural self-determination, through love for self and others; through his recognition that his and his people's mission, in conjunction with the world's other peoples, is to bring into being a *new* World Order. This new order must not be a "colored" version of the old and present Eurocentric order which has inspired his criminalization and the dehumanization of mankind, but one inspired by his own remembrance and full psychic integration.

White America's Perception of Black America's Attitudes toward Crime

The African American community is stereotypically perceived by the White American community as "soft on crime." This perception seems to imply that African Americans evince a higher tolerance for criminality, are more willing to rationalize and excuse criminal behavior, support more lenient sentencing and treatment of those convicted of crimes — especially African American offenders — than do European Americans. This perception by European Americans of the African American community's attitudes toward crime, particularly "street crime," is intriguing in view of the fact that the African American community is victimized to a far greater extent than is the European American community. This stereotypical perception of African American attitudes toward "street crime" seems emblematic of reverse psychology used to produce the most important adjunctive rationalizations of White American domination of African peoples. In this instance White Americans, who are by far significantly less affected by Black "street crime," project themselves as its most frequent victims, and create the perception of their communities as being the most threatened by violent Black criminals and Black instigated "street crime" in general. The stereotypical public image of "street crime" is one of Black culprit and White victim.

The stereotypical perception of Whites as the most frequent victims of Black instigated criminal assaults and other activities despite facts to the contrary, is aided and abetted by those most efficient repressive instruments of the White American collective ego responsible for the ego-defensive denial and distortion of reality and psychopathological stereotyping of African Americans — the White American media in conjunction with the White American entertainment industry. The White American press stridently and untiringly reports the victimization of Whites by Black criminals, while not reporting or at best, under-reporting, Black victimization by Black or White criminals, or White victimization by White criminals. Nearly *ninety* percent of crimes committed against Whites are committed by Whites. The White dominated entertainment industry profits greatly from the presentation of Blacks as criminals and malefactors of all types. The stereotypical image of "Black criminal/White victim," is apparently utilized by the White American community to deny its own criminal and violent history, its current criminality and violent victimization of others, as well as to justify its economic and political oppression of African Americans by various means. These means include: the use of draconian police methods; police brutality; violation and suspension of due process; double-standard sentencing of African American convicts; the imprisonment of Black males more for prejudicial and political reasons than for their objectively determined criminal behavior; the harassment and imprisonment of Black males who have not committed crimes; the creating and maintaining of the socioeconomic and psychosocial motivating conditions conducive to the production of African American criminality and violent antisocial behavior.]

There is a reluctance on the part of the African American community to turn over its alleged Black-on-Black or Black-on-White victimizers to an alien, colonial, occupying and brutal police force; a force which indiscriminately treats African American "law-abiding" citizens and criminal offenders alike. Its realistic ambivalence toward the criminal court and criminal justice system which blatantly violates due process and the civil rights of Blacks, its reluctance to go along with what it knows is a White community conspiracy to criminalize and often falsely accuse its sons and daughters and subject them to unjust and abusive corrections practices, is characterized by the White community as indicative of the African American community's tendency to easily tolerate or to "coddle" or sympathize with criminals. This is also the case when the African American community humanistically demands that Black defendants, regardless of their innocence or guilt, be treated fairly, and be presumed innocent until proven guilty instead of presumed guilty by merely having been arrested, indicted, or called before the court. The African American community's demand that even if guilty, Black arrestees, detainees and prisoners not be subjected to unnecessary force, defenselessly shot to death, or otherwise unnecessarily psychologically and physically abused, is characterized as condoning Black criminality by the White American community.

If it unwittingly cooperates with an historically and contemporary crimogenic White-dominated society, White racist police force, criminal (in)justice establishment and correction system, the African American community allies itself with its racist enemies, opposes its own communal interests, and abets its degradation and destruction. However, when it does not cooperate with the antagonistic White racist establishment in protecting itself from its criminal element, it is made to appear to be tolerant of their presence and condoning of their activities and the victimization of itself. More importantly, it appears to collusively cooperate with its criminal elements in dismantling, destabilizing, disorganizing, and ultimately destroying itself and society. It is thereby made to appear to be essentially criminal in nature and principally concerned with criminally victimizing the White community. Caught in this no-win position the African American community consequently becomes paralyzed or indecisive, lukewarmly committed, or seemingly indifferent and unresponsive to State sponsored (*read*: White American sponsored) ostensibly "crime prevention" programs, which, like many other White American rehabilitation programs are elaborate covers and rationales for all-out assaults on its integrity and well-being.

3

AMERICAN SOCIETY —

CRIMOGENIC SOCIETY

> If we are not to speak of individuals as criminal, can we
> then refer to a criminal society? ...I think we can describe
> our society as criminal — indeed I think we must.
>
> — EDWIN M. SCHUR
> *Our Criminal Society*

HUMAN BEHAVIOR regardless of type, like other forms of behavior, can only be defined and understood in relative terms. Human behavior only reflects meaning relative to the behavior of other human beings and can best be understood in terms of human relations. Criminal behavior is human behavior. It is social behavior. It is not delimited, discontinuous, and individual as is typically implied by "established" social scientists. The individual, the subgroup or subculture, are individual or collective only in the sense that they uniquely represent the social history, experience, socialized perspectives, values, and behavioral expressions endemic to a social system as a whole. Individuals, subgroups and the social systems in which they exist and with which they interact are continuous; each mutually defining the other, each interdependently interpenetrating the other; each to some very significant degree helping to shape the other. In the individual, in the group, we see the social system

33

as uniquely represented by that individual or group. In him or it we see the system of social-political relations in microcosm.

Black American criminality whether in its individual or subgroup form, is a microcosmic reflection of the macrocosmic American system and beyond that, of the system of European global domination. The intrapsychic motivational orientation of the Black American individual or subgroup is driven and structured by the nature of his or its social-political, ecological encounters with European Americans and Europeans in general. These encounters are not ones between equals, nor are they ones characterized by mutual respect and reciprocity. These frontiers of disparate intergroup encounter are the nodal points at which both Black criminals and Black "law-abiding" citizens are produced. They are both Eurocentric creations as are the nature and quality of their social relations and functions. In this context, the Black American criminal is "law-abiding," obeying the laws of the Eurocentric criminalization process. Black criminality is not accidental, coincidental or aberrant, but speaks to an apparent need in the White American community to induce criminality in a significant proportion of the Black American community, as well as its need to perceive African Americans as innately criminal, just as it exhibits the related need to perceive the average African American as innately intellectually inferior.

The Criminalization of the Black Male

In light of the foregoing and of the forthcoming, we must recognize that within limits, alleged Black crime is socioeconomically functional for the White American status quo and is ultimately symptomatic of the societal "needs" of powerful segments of the American class structure and of its dysfunctionality. In this context, we must ask and answer the following questions: Why do White Americans need to criminalize significant segments of the African American population? What is the sociopolitical function of alleged African American criminality and self-destructive behavior in American society? How does alleged Black American criminality sustain the American status quo? How is "criminal motivation" induced into the personalities and social relations of some African Americans and for what reasons? While the scope of this book will not allow us to adequately deal with these questions, they must be answered and the answers pragmatically utilized if the alleged criminality, self-destructiveness, and victimization of African Americans are to be eradicated in Black American communities.

The rates of Black-on-Black homicidal violence, assault and victimization, though biased and inaccurate, are alarming. The percentages cited in the prior chapter say something ominously significant, not only about the collective character of Black America, but all the more so about the collective character of White America. The percentages in the prior chapter have been used by a very significant and influential proportion of White America to stereotypically assassinate the character of the collective African personality in general, and to indict the Black American male as innately criminal in particular.

In the eyes of White America, an exaggeratedly large segment of Black America is criminally suspect. This is especially true relative to the Black American male. In the fevered mind of White America he is cosmically guilty. His guilt is existential. For him to be alive is to be suspected, to be stereotypically accused, convicted and condemned for criminal conspiracy and intent. On the streets, in the subways, elevators, parks, in the "wrong" neighborhood, from late childhood to late adulthood, he is feared, suspiciously scrutinized, cautiously approached or warily avoided.

To be a sensitive Black male, no matter how innocent, law-abiding, all-American, patriotic, altruistic, and loving, is to see the dilated pupils of fear in White women's and old men's eyes, to witness the defensive clutching at pocketbooks, to see yourself reflected in the mirrors of the other's eyes as a mugger, thief, and rapist. To be a perceptive Black male is to look out at an accusative world and feel oneself the object of a suspicious ocular examination by trigger-happy policemen, to have your papers checked by security personnel while your White counterpart passes the checkpoint without question. To be a Black male is to have your integrity chronically under question, to always have to somehow verbally or nonverbally, communicate convincing reasons for being where you are if you are not in your "place." Only the carefully presented facade, the meticulous expression of nonaggressive, nonassertive body language, the representation of a carefully managed nonthreatening persona, or old age; only standardized, "non-Black" dress, standardized English, averted eyes intently focused on the leading newspaper, magazine, or book can alleviate to some tolerable degree the fears and suspicions of others. But this diminution of fear and suspiciousness in others bought at the too-high price of self-annihilation, is always tentative, delicate, and is easily rent by the smallest misstep or the tiniest deviation.

Given the historical and contemporary virulence of White racism in America and the injustice toward Blacks that such racism engenders, the number of arrests, incarcerations, and in many instances, convictions of Black males should be viewed with a jaundiced eye. [The willingness of White Americans to heavily tax themselves in order to finance accelerated and increased prison construction, rapidly expanding police forces and so-called criminal justice system personnel, burgeoning private police and security establishments; their willingness to finance the incarceration of a Black male prisoner upwards of $30,000 to $40,000 per year, in sharp contrast to their unwillingness to tax themselves to provide for the appropriate funding of the education of Black children and to commit themselves to the ending of racist employment practices; to provide adequate housing medical care, food and clothing; clearly implies that alleged Black male criminality plays a very important role in defining the collective White American ego and personality.]

The typical White American response to the so-called criminality of the Black male when closely examined, clearly indicates that it is more consistent with a conscious and unconscious need to instigate and sustain Black criminality as a highly visible and publicized component of American society, than with a yearning to reduce its destructive influence on both Black and White societies. White America needs an expressly "hyped" Black American criminality the way a neurotic patient needs his symptoms, despite his protests to the contrary. In other words, the existence of Black American criminality, alleged and actual, is a political-economic, social-psychological necessity for maintaining White American psychical and material equilibrium. Black American criminality apparently serves fundamental Eurocentric psychopolitical needs and is engendered and sustained for this reason. We will now examine some of these needs.

White American Paranoia

To look at the world or a segment of it with a rigid, hyper-alert, and all-consuming expectation — to search reality repetitively only for confirmation of one's suspicions while ignoring aspects of that reality which disconfirm those suspicions; to pay no attention to opposing rational arguments, cogent, well-founded evidence, except to find in them only those features that seem to confirm one's original views; to examine reality with extraordinary prejudice, rejecting facts, information and alternative possibilities while seizing on and exaggerating any scintilla of often irrelevant evidence that supports one's original expectations — denotes a driven need: a psychoneurotic, psychopathological need to defend an ego perilously in danger of disintegration and to defend it regardless of cost to oneself and others. Such a suspicious and paranoid orientation speaks to the need to rigidly construct and control reality so as to maintain self-control, to empower the ego and to gainfully exploit a relevant situation. This rigidity of attention, stereotypical viewing of the world; this chronic condition of hyper-alertness, hypersensitivity; this need to create the world according to one's own deluded images, to subject others to one's paranoid views, to exploitatively have them serve that need, bespeaks the greater need to gain ego satisfaction and enhancement, self-definition and material gain through manipulating the behavior and consciousness over others. Paradoxically, this greater need bespeaks a fundamental dependency on a world and others and simultaneously, of a protest against and denial of that dependency. It expresses an ego vulnerability which must remain defensively hidden, an ego weakness which must appear to itself and others as strength, an extremely tense, unstable ego whose tenuous equilibrium can only be maintained by projecting that tension and vulnerability into the world and others. Thus the keeper of law comes to need the outlaw. And needing him, creates him. The keeper of the disturbs the peace by projecting hallucinated hostile threats where they do not exist.

That the White American must see virtually every Black male as criminal or as a potential criminal regardless of facts to the contrary, bespeaks an intense psychic need of White America to perceive him as such.

What does White America have to gain from choosing to perceive Black males as stereotypically criminal? By socio-psychologically inducing Black males into criminality? Following the trend of thought set forth by Michael Lewis in his book, *The Culture of Inequality*, alleged Black male criminality is a comfort to White America despite its protestations to the contrary. Alleged Black criminality, while evoking White American fear and loathing, reassures them of their vaunted self-worth, their assumed innately superior moral standing, of their self-congratulatory self-constraint in contrast with presumed Black American unworthiness, innate inferior moral standing, inherent criminality, lack of self-constraint and self-control. White America's self-appreciation is enhanced as it insatiably feeds on overblown reports about Black criminality while denying its own incomparable criminal record, and its own racist-imperialist incubation and giving birth to the very same criminal forces which now threaten to destroy it.

Black criminals function as a *negative reference group* vital to maintaining the White American self-image. The Black criminal is used to support the White American community's self-serving, self-justifying judgments of itself. White America's preoccupation with Black criminality betrays its own need for reassurance; betrays its own basic insecurity regarding its projected moral purity. Consequently, the higher the incidence of reported Black criminality, the more exceptionally righteous White America feels itself to be. The more righteous it feels itself to be the more intensely and guiltlessly it promulgates and justifies its domination and exploitation of African peoples at home and abroad. The alleged innate criminality of Black America, particularly of Black males, and their actual high level of self-destructive criminality remain incontrovertible psycho-political necessities if the White American-Eurocentric culture of inequality is to be self-justifiably continued without end. In the context of this collective necessity, more Blacks are arrested, charged, tried, convicted, and sentenced to longer prison terms for allegedly committing the same type of crimes as Whites. Many are arrested, charged, tried, convicted and sentenced to long prison terms merely for committing the crime of being Black in America.

The White American community's need to stereotypically perceive Blacks as innately criminal, coupled with its socioeconomic power to control the availability of resources and their renumerative allocation, confers on it the power of creating or controlling circumstances conducive to the satisfaction of its hegemonic requirements. Under these circumstances, the need of the collective White ego to project an image of endemic Black criminality in order to maintain its power status quo, is tantamount to the creation of Black criminality, particularly of the self-destructive kind.

The Black Male as Potential Rebel

Whether as the result of acculturation or of innate biological propensities, when a community perceives itself to be the object of oppression or perceives its vital institutions and members to be at risk such that decisive actions must be taken, the males traditionally undertake leadership of the resistance. Males and the bonding between them in coalition with their female counterparts, form the backbone of a viable society. Significant males are essential to a community's intra-dependence, structure, social coherence, continuity, viability, adaptability, self-defense and liberation from oppression and exploitation. Traditionally, the male component of an exploited community is seen by its exploiters, who themselves are usually males, as by temperament and biological/cultural endowment, the most likely to take up arms both psychosocially and/or materially against its oppressors. Consequently, oppressors typically target the male component of the oppressed community for relatively more intense repression, containment, imprisonment, humiliation, emasculation, socio-political-economic discrimination, personality assassination, and various forms of physical eradication. The neutralization of an oppressed community's males by the destruction of their character, authority and credibility, allows an oppressor to override that society's territorial and institutional imperatives and exposes it to unrestrained, rapacious domination and exploitation. Consequently, the institutional and organizational integrity of the oppressed community becomes dysfunctional or nonfunctional and the community is thereupon destructively exploited by aliens and/or is left to self-destruct. Emasculated males under such circumstances may become unwitting allies to, and vehicles of, the genocide and suicide of their community. These eviscerated, uprooted males may inadvertently become instruments of oppression by preying on their own community, thwarting its viable interests instead of defending them. Thus, the psychological disarmament of male resistance results in the destructive exploitation of the community against which that male resistance would ordinarily fight.

The psychopolitical need of White America to dominate Black America in a variety of ways requires that it neutralizes by any means necessary, any type of Black male empowerment, actual or potential, which may threaten its hegemony. Two of these means involve the criminalization of the Black male and of the Black community in general. The criminalization of the Black male by White America immensely enhances its psychocultural and material advantages. Criminalization of the Black male and the African American community in general by the White American community, psychopolitically benefits the latter community in a myriad of ways including the following:

- Justification of the proscription of the liberties African peoples through continuing oppression, denial of civil and other human rights, and justification of racial discrimination and segregation.

- Justification of the power status quo by utilizing the alleged criminality of the Black community to rationalize severe police repression, social and employment discrimination, restriction of African American political activity and empowerment, civil liberties, constitutional guarantees of individual and communal self-defense, and self-definition.

- Facilitation of White American economic control of the African American community by frustrating and removing potential economic competition from the exploited African American community by denying it access to economic resources, distorting and thwarting its economic developmental potentials. This economic control effectively neutralizes the ability of the African American community to lead the worldwide African community in challenging worldwide Eurocentric politicoeconomic hegemony.

- Provision of rationalizations for a collective White American preemptive strike against feared African economic, cultural, and more importantly, military parity — by aggressively attacking its potentiality on the ground through the self-serving manipulation, constriction, and undermining of the political, educational, economical, cultural institutions as well as experiences important for African American self-development and independence.

• Creation of interpersonal/intragroup fear, suspicion, mistrust, violence, and lack of self-respect within the Black community, enabling destabilizing and destructive forces to vitiate its corporate identity, cohesive unity, and its ability to benefit from its own wealth and protect its autonomous liberty. This mission is most efficiently accomplished and sustained if the created fears, etc., appear to flow from factors culturally endemic to the African community and reflective of the supposed inferior personality propensities innately characteristic of African peoples.

• Creation of "social service" and "criminal justice" *industries*. The "criminal justice" system is best understood as a multi-billion dollar industry wherein the African American male is utilized as its basic raw material, the processing and the "refining" of which provides income for White families, vendors, construction firms, professionals, law and security enforcement agencies. Thus, alleged Black male criminality plays an important vital economic role in many White American communities. For this reason it is highly unlikely that these communities will seriously commit themselves to rectification of those social conditions which instigate and sustain alleged Black criminality and to the negation of those systematic injustices which underpin a White-controlled penal/economic fiefdom.

• Justification for the atrocities it historically, currently, and in the future shall continue to perpetuate against the American African community. By ascribing an inherent criminality to African peoples just as it ascribes to these same peoples an alleged inherent intellectual inferiority, the White American community can, through ego-defensive projection and other ego defense mechanisms, deny its role in creating, maintaining, and benefitting from the negative condition of the African American community, and of African people in general.

- Provision of an underpinning for White communal self-definition, self-image, ego-support, self-aggrandizement and positive self-feeling by elevating itself while denigrating African peoples, vicariously enjoying their relative deprivation, alleged depravity, and visible subordination. The absence of perceived African inferiority in all its varieties would bring into question the illusory European superiority complex, destroy European self-confidence and related rationales for the hegemonic domination and exploitation of African peoples in America and abroad.

A perceived high level of Black criminal activity, especially if confined to the African American community, provides both primary and secondary gains for the White American collective ego complex. Therefore, any program which can effectively erase the criminal image of the Black male and reduce his self-destructive criminality will most likely not be forthcoming from the White community despite its pretensions to the contrary. Moreover, any effective crime control programs instituted by the African American community (the place from which any effective program must issue or gain substantial support) will be by deliberate design, stealth, or neglect, targeted for neutralization by an apparently "well-meaning" White community.

4

THE CREATION OF
THE BLACK CRIMINAL

Yet some people are selected to occupy the status "criminal." Usually this happens because they are thought to have acted in ways that threaten the interests embodied in the law. Criminalization thus involves the application of criminal law to a person's behavior. *Insofar as the criteria for labeling someone a "criminal" reflect some disparity in group interests and power, that which is defined as crime and those who are selected to fill the criminal status are socially created objects of the structural characteristics of human society that produce conflict and an inequitable distribution of power in society.*

— Clayton A. Hartjen
Crime and Criminalization

A self-fulfilling prophecy is an assumption or pre-diction that, purely as a result of having been made, causes the expected or predicted event to occur and thus confirms its own "accuracy."

— Paul Watzlawick
The Invented Reality

When men define situations as real, they are real in their consequences."

— W.I. Thomas (in Watzlawick)

The Criminalization of the Black Community

A PARABLE: A man named John once owned a show dog who had won for his master many prizes, helped him to become wealthy, win the envy of his friends, and even helped to save his master's life on a number of occasions. As the vicissitudes of capitalism would have it, there came a time when there was no longer any money in the show dog business. This situation changed Master John's feelings toward his once prized possession. He could be heard often saying — "He is lazy, a good-for-nothing cur. All he wants to do is just lie around and eat-up my food. I wish he'd just go away." Filled with hatred and resentment, Master John, by various cruel and ingenious means, drove his dog rabidly mad.

One day as fate would deign it, the mad dog attempted to attack its master. Master John felled him with a single shot from his elephant gun. Because there was a law against shooting dogs Master John was tried before a jury of his peers. Master John as represented by his lawyer pleaded self-defense — "It is cut and dried," his lawyer exhorted! "The dog was mad and in his madness he sought to attack his master, who in self-defense, shot him. His driving the dog mad and thus allegedly having precipitated the dog's attack as argued by the prosecutor is irrelevant and immaterial! Has not a man the right of self-defense? Besides, he was only a dog prone by dog-nature to go mad. Had he not been a dog he would not have been driven mad in the first place! For, if his master had not shot him the dog would have lived to attack one of us, our wives, our elders, our fair-haired little children. What does it matter how he became mad? What does it matter if one mad dog is no longer disturbing the peace and posing a threat to law and order? Master John did the world a favor. For that we should honor him, not persecute him." The jury of his peers found him not guilty.

Thus began the strange career of Master John whose single--minded purpose in life became that of breeding mad dogs and executing them in self-defense. He thereby gained great reputation and honored status among his neighbors who he protected from mad dogs running loose in the streets. He became an expert at breeding, apprehending, and executing mad dogs. To increase yield and therewith his remuneration — for this was by now a very lucrative business — he penned his trained mad dogs in with the not-so-mad dogs, many of whom themselves became mad and in escaping their confines, threatened the peace. Mad dogs were everywhere. The neighbors in their fear and terror became incapable of distinguishing the mad dogs from the not-so-mad dogs. All dogs, even the ones who were "members of the family" — even Cassie, the model dog, who everyone thought was near-human — aroused their suspicions. Thus as a preventative measure the village was lamentably forced to liquidate all dogs, regardless of their social status or mental state. After all, a dog is a dog, is a dog. They even formed a society for the eradication of all dogs everywhere. That is why on any quiet night of the week you can no longer hear a single dog baying at the full moon in Canineville today.

THE CRIMINAL IS one to whom an opprobrious label has been successfully attached. Labeling not only prescribes the behavior of others toward the one labeled criminal, or only negatively seeks to characterize him. It also tends to transform his self-concept and behavior in such ways that incarnates or substantiates the criminal appellation.

If to be criminalized, especially when the objective basis for such a designation does not exist, is to be dehumanized and to be related to as such by "significant others," then the criminalization of the African American male can be arguably said to have begun with the need of White Americans to justify their enslavement of Africans, and continues concomitant with their need to capitalize on unending African politico-economic subordination.

The cursing (a form of labeling) of another is tantamount to his dehumanization. It is usually a ritualistic prelude and justification for the other's subordination, or assault, or murder of another. The criminalization of Black people, particularly of the Black male, is a prelude for the rationalization of his economic exploitation, and ultimately, a prelude to the Eurocentric murder of the African population.

The American Dilemma

In its oppression of Black America, White America faces a major dilemma. The White ruling class seeks to project a self-image and public image which are liberal and nonviolent. It wishes to assume the appearance of being faithfully committed to protecting the constitutional and civil rights guarantees of all residents — regardless of race, color, creed, or condition of previous servitude — and to be perceived by them as inherently humane. At the same time the ruling class wishes to retain its power to rule, to maintain its tremendous wealth, power, hegemony and privileges. Thus it is confronted with a major contradiction: it cannot actualize its projected image and commitments without destroying the bases of its identity and power. Since this class is not committed to its own destruction we must logically infer that its projected self-image, public image, and sociopolitical commitments are false and hypocritical. Social equality and privilege across classes and ethnocultural groups cannot exist simultaneous with White American sociopolitical and economic dominance. Class privilege and advantage require the subordination of other classes and groups. For these reasons, American institutions operate in opposition to their publicized missions when dealing with the underclasses and subordinated groups. Consequently, the major social institutions which seek to project an image of objectivity and neutrality, in actuality operate in the oppressive interests of the society's ruling groups and against the interests of its subordinate groups.

In sum, the ruling groups cannot maintain their hegemony and sustain socioeconomic inequality, which are the foundations of their regency, without perverting the ostensible missions of the society's sociopolitical institutions and utilizing them as instruments of oppression. In America this perversion must take place while the ruling groups hide their oppressive faces behind the seductive facade of democracy, liberty, equality, and brotherhood.

Hence, when we look at major American institutions relative to African Americans, we observe the following reversals: the economic system keeps them poor; the criminal justice system mediates injustice; the educational establishment creates ignorance and intellectual incompetence; the family institution breeds broken homes and "illegitimate" children; the health and welfare system catalyzes sickness and administers health-care neglect (*the life-span of African Americans is actually decreasing*); and the religious institutions support the immorality of racial injustice. These institutions are designed to deceive, fashioned to seem ameliorative while actually aiding and abetting the injurious exploitation of the populations they are supposedly commissioned to help. Paradoxically, they must appear to uplift while in reality maintain, and if necessary, intensify suppression. In fact, their apparent uplifting efforts must in actuality be disguised forms of oppression and annihilation. Their ameliorative ideology and practice must be endemically opposed to the interests of the subordinate classes and groups while appearing otherwise.

In the context of the American dilemma the socioeconomic immobilization and destruction of the African American population must occur most intensely at the very time when a minuscule segment of that population appears to be garnering increased social and political status, and when a very substantial percentage of African Americans are deceived into thinking that such increasing status is indicative of "Black progress." Racist agendas must be pressed while the dominant White groups for the most part, appear to be less overtly racist in attitude and behavior. Thus, if necessary, African American genocide must occur during the time the ruling segments of the White American citizenry seem to be relatively most committed to African American survival, upliftment, complete social, political and economic assimilation into the mythical "American mainstream."

Hence the American ruling class dilemma: How must the required oppression, and if need be, genocidal elimination of African Americans and African peoples, be accomplished by the ruling class without it appearing to have instigated and perpetuated their oppression and elimination? How can African Americans be made to suffer negation of their political, economic, social, and albeit, their biological existence, without that negation appearing to be the work of the collective White community and its allied hosts?

Practical answers to these questions require that the continuing oppression and/or genocidal annihilation of the African American population by White America be accomplished through deliberate psychopolitical subterfuge, or through use of the collective ego defensive method of unconsciously programming and executing African American oppression and annihilation while consciously appearing not to do otherwise. In actuality, the collective White ego complex utilizes both methods.

Through the use of projection, reaction formation, rationalization and other collective ego defenses, White America magically makes its genocidal destruction of the African American community appear to be the result of African American self-destruction. In *reaction formation* the individual, and in this instance, a collectivity, represses and retains in the subconscious undesirable impulses and attitudes, and assumes personally conscious and public attitudes and behaviors diametrically opposed to those unconscious orientations. In the practice of rationalization the individual or the collectivity, in order to prevent the conscious and public revelation and the taking of responsibility for unacceptable motives, concocts reasons which superficially appear to be "true" while not indeed being so. Rationalization is perhaps the most frequently used psychodynamic mechanism of reality distortion. Through these collective ego defense mechanisms the social, political, economic, moral and physical demise of Black America is made to appear in the collective mind of White America to be the suicidal result of alleged African American predispositions, innate inabilities, disabilities, incompetencies, venalities, and a host of other personality and collective flaws that have nothing to do with White American oppression.

The fact that motives may be denied, distorted, or submerged in the unconscious, or may be intentionally but self-servingly rationalized, does not rob them of their capacity to be actualized in reality. Unconscious programs can be, and are more often than not, methodically carried out in reality. Unconsciousness of a program merely permits its conscious agent or executive to deny its existence, intentionality, and his instrumentality. The agent in this case can, with "good conscience," deny culpability for performing an act which, if admitted, would make him justifiably subject to condemnation and penalization. The victim of the agent's activities must be blamed. To be blamed in "good conscience" by a victimizing agent, the victim ideally must, in ways hidden and unconscious to both perpetrator and victim, have his collective modal personality and social relations so organized and orchestrated, his history and future so distorted, his identity and sense of purpose so structured, that he comes to harbor and express apparently self-destructive and antisocial tendencies. Utilized by the White American community, ego defensive traits and tendencies are the unconscious instruments for the continuing oppression, or in the extreme, annihilation of the African American community.

To achieve "self-destruction" at the subliminal behest of White America, the African American population must be unconsciously programmed by the White American community to mount a deadly assault upon itself and annihilate itself by its own hands. Its self-annihilation must be both violent and insidious. The conscious and unconscious programming of Black America by White America also involves the organization and expression of African American behavior which is "antisocial," thereby requiring suppression by the White American police state. What better way to *provoke* "deadly but necessary" violence against the African American community than first to criminalize that community and then execute it for its alleged criminality?

Alienation of the African American Personality

Black-on-Black crime, with Black males acting as erstwhile suicidal, fratricidal *Manchurian candidates* or mercenaries who unwittingly have been recruited to execute the continuing White American hegemonic assault on the African American community, necessarily requires that their personalities be psychologically conditioned and transformed to play their "assigned" roles by the Eurocentric establishment. Moreover, it requires that these personalities be made unconsciously responsive to, and malleably compatible with, White American imperialistic needs. These robotized rangers must be extrinsically motivated by White American manufactured desires and commodities. All-in-all, in order that the African American community appear to be intrinsically incompetent, incoherent, threatening, dangerously criminal, dependent and prone to self-destruction, a sizeable segment of its population must be criminally "alienated," that is, made host to White American introjectively structured behavioral tendencies which are compatible with White American hegemonic interests.

Alienation of the African personality requires a psychotechnological creative process, a process imperial Europeans know well. The Eurocentric alienation of the captive African personality is achieved by a variety of methods, including manipulation of the African American experiential/informational context, the use of conditioning, associative learning, i.e., the reinforced association of African cultural, ethnic and personal characteristics with other negative and undesirable characteristics. In seeking to dissociate himself from those negatively associated and falsified African images, the African American escapes and dissociates from any identification with true, positive and liberating African images which the falsified images obscure. The White American community severely *punishes* through social ostracism, ridicule, mockery, employment discrimination, physical assault and denial of fundamental *civil rights*, those African Americans who openly identify with and espouse African culture, history, values, autonomy and liberation. African Americans who demonstrate an apparent rejection of their African identity, African culture, history and values, and acknowledge their subordination to European domination, are rewarded with increased opportunities, material and social compensation, although restricted relative to White Americans. By these and other methods, the oppressed African American is alienated from the possibility of developing a functionally realistic perception of reality, knowledge of self, self-control, self-esteem, self-acceptance, positive self-feeling, ability to form affectionate and practical social relationships with other African Americans, and identification with an undistorted positive African cultural and ethnic image. The Eurocentric psychopolitical, socioeconomic domination of African peoples is founded and sustained by its historical and current perversion of these characteristics.

The Eurocentric process of alienating the collective African American personality, (i.e., making it responsively compatible with Eurocentric interests), effectively begins with Eurocentric control over African American psychoecological, psychocultural, socioeconomical, psychopolitical and bio-social existence. Eurocentric control over conditions vital to the quality and extent of African American psychophysical existence is manipulatively utilized to falsify the African heritage, image, and characterization. Under these circumstances Africans are either forced to identify with, or feel compelled to, compensatorily and/or dissociatively, escape from their negatively ascribed Africanicity by the assuming of various eurocentrically oriented *alien* identities. These eurocentrically introjected and motivated identities, misperceived by African Americans as representing who they innately and intrinsically are, are the instrumental psychomechanisms by which African American self-perception, personal and interpersonal relations, and collective sociopolitical goals are manipulated in favor of European domination. These identities are supremely responsive to White American programmatic input (other non-European aliens also can and do manipulatively program them to a lesser, but significant extent). They permit the White American interactive programming of the collective African American personality to the point of motivating the apparently self-mediated destruction of the African individual and communal self at the occult behest of their Eurocentric programmers.

White American Self-fulfilling Prophecies and Falsifications of the African Personality

The White American falsified African identity is introjected, actualized and interactively programmed within the body and ego complex of the collective African personality principally by means of projective self-fulfilling processes. White American projectively-based exploitation of African Americans would not be psychodynamically successful if the exploited African ego complex could present an effectively opposing set of cognitive, personal, and behavioral characteristics which would belie them. In order for the White American exploitation of African Americans to achieve psychodynamic and material success, it is necessary that eurocentrically falsified images, thoughts and behavioral orientations be actualized in the collective African American psyche. This actualized projection is utilized by the White American ruling class complex to exploitatively influence and shape collective African American cognitive styles, physiological and spiritual functionality, self-perception, perception of reality, social relations, experiential history, and appetitive strivings.

Paraphrasing the leading quotation at the beginning of this chapter, one may define a *self-fulfilling prophecy* as a projective assumption or prediction which, as a result of having been authoritatively projected, causes the projected assumption or prediction to be realized, thereby confirming its own "accuracy." The projective self-fulfilling prophecy becomes fulfilled because the act of prophesying itself prescribes actions on the part of the prophet who creates and sustains the conditions necessary to bring into being the expected event; because actions on the part of the projecting party create and sustain a conditioned reality which would not have arisen had not the prophecy been made in the first place. Thus, the projective prophecy dynamically produces its own reality, actuality and "truth." This conditioned reality is channelized, created, formed and bounded by a set of projectively organized and regulated actions and interactions on the part of the projecting party. That is, the prophet or projecting party first makes a prediction or expresses an expectation regarding his target person or group. If powerful, he then arranges the life conditions and experiences of his target, in accordance with his predictions and expectations. The target, in adapting to the conditions or relations imposed on him by the prophet or projecting party, and in reacting emotionally to those conditions, is often conditioned and shaped to think and behave in ways compatible with the power interests of the projecting party. Additionally, the target's character and personality, his thinking and emotional orientations and abilities, reflect the conditioning imposed on him by the projecting party or prophet. Hence, the target fulfills the initial predictions or prophecies of the projectionist.

Internalization of White Racism by African Americans

The Eurocentric projective self-fulfilling prophecy can only be actualized with the unwitting collusive participation of its intended victim, the African American population. The introjection of eurocentrically falsified African images into the collective African American personality can only occur when African Americans themselves accept those falsified images as fact. Only when the lie is accepted as truth, only when a false projection is seen as a fact by virtue of its having been put forth by the ultimate validators of truth and reality, the ruling White Americans, can it be internalized and utilized by targeted African Americans to accordingly structure their personalities and interpersonal relations in ways that permit White American projected expectations to fulfill themselves.

This acceptance of false images by African Americans is made all the more easy and efficient by the fact that information, whether true or untrue, is almost completely controlled and manipulated by White American academic and propaganda establishments. Information which belies the stereotypical and "accepted" views of African history and culture, which refute false perceptions of the African personality and mental capability, were and are, severely repressed by the White American psycho-political establishment. With no alternative information readily available to it, or having such information invalidated by the White American academic establishment and press, the African American community was and is left to fall under the influence of negative Eurocentric stereotypes. Consequently, many in it seek to alienate themselves from anything African, seek to identify with White Americans and other ethnic groups. Others, by various maladjustive means, seek to escape the "curse" of being born black.

Hence, a combination of exploitative White American projective self-fulfilling prophecies and related actions relative to the African American community, in conjunction with African American credulity, actualize within the collective African American psyche a falsified and painfully negative "self-image." The identification with, or attempted avoidance of, the existence of that negative image generates and sustains a variety of maladjustive, reactionary personality/communal lifestyles and orientations which aid and abet the domination of the African American community by White Americans.

It should be noted here that the discovery of and identification with a true and positive basal African self-image is severely punished or negatively reinforced by the ruling White American establishment which recognizes that such an identification would provide a basis for the liberation of African Americans from White ruling-class control and exploitation. Additionally, such an identification with a positive African self-image by African Americans, if widespread, would challenge and very possibly overthrow the White American socioeconomic, political hegemonic establishment. Consequently, the existence and active acceptance of a basically positive and realistic African identity must be obliterated, must be associated by the White American establishment with withdrawal of its paternalistic "affection" for African Americans, associated with pain and possible annihilation, thereby making movement toward such identification on the part of African Americans vulnerable to overwhelming conscious and unconscious anxiety attacks.

The reactionary "taking root" within the collective African American psyche of falsified personality formations or orientations supportive of its exploitative domination by others, particularly White Americans, requires that each African American internalizes and acts out negative attitudes toward other African Americans. The reactionary African American then becomes prone to expressing the same or similar attitudes and behaviors toward his fellow victims and himself as they are expressed toward him by his White American oppressors. At this point he identifies with his oppressor and unwittingly enters into an alliance with him to exploitatively suppress the optimal adaptive viability of his own ethnic group.

This self-alienating internalization of negative attitudes toward himself and his group and his identification with his White American oppressors by the reactionary African American, is motivated by the false assumption that his plight is caused by the "color of his skin," by his innate African-ness, and not the depravity of his oppressors. Furthermore, he believes that it is his White oppressors' attitudes toward African peoples and their apparent power to willfully abuse and exploit them that are the most salient evidence of their superiority, of their "non-niggerness" and of the "niggerness" of African peoples. Therefore he comes to believe that his own attitudinal and behavioral treatment of other Africans as they are treated by their White oppressors is evidence of his own "non-niggerness", of his own non-Africanness, which in effect makes him an ersatz or "honorary" White. While in the "average or bourgeois" African American such internalization and identification processes lead to the development of unauthentic personality formations which become the source of self-defeating self-concepts and social/communal/political relations, those African Americans who have deeply internalized Eurocentric attitudes toward themselves and others like themselves, may actualize those attitudes in the form of violent homicidal assaults on other "niggers" and/or in the form of self-destructive assaults on themselves. Thus, the violent Black criminal who attacks another Black as the result of a relatively minor incident, or when the objective basis for such an attack does not exist, is one whose internalized rage toward what he has been inductively made to perceive himself, and others like himself to be, is so intense until only violent outbursts against others perceived to be like himself can relieve the pressure. He thereby becomes the salient symbol in the White American mind of innate Black criminality and a handy vehicle for substantiating the alleged criminality of the African American community.

To summarize, *internalization* refers to the process whereby a subject as the result of conditioning, exposure to certain types of information, definitions and interpretations of reality, deliberately restricted experiences and opportunities, observational learning and imitation, fantasies, and other incentives, as manipulated by certain influential persons or groups, comes to incorporate into his active belief, behavioral, and evaluative systems, the values; attitudes and lifestyles characteristic of such persons and groups. Negative internalization occurs when the values, mores, etc., are introjected by the internalizing subject in such ways as to cause him to behave maladaptively or self-destructively.

The internalization of values, beliefs, doctrines, and such, as represented by accepted authorities, prestigious persons and groups, is utilized by the targeted subject as a frame of reference within which he may act, expect to receive gratification, and critically judge the behavior and motivations of others as well as himself. Internalization provides the basis for the construction of the targeted subject's conscience, goals and interests, cognitive and learning styles, as well as rationalizations for his behavior toward others and himself.

Negative internalization of values, attitudes, doctrines etc., as presented by certain authority figures, even if the acceptance of such attitudes and values compels the internalizer to perceive himself negatively (e.g., a negative self-concept, low self-esteem), is more likely to occur in the situations where the internalizer is dependent on those authority figures, is paternalistically related to them, feels he needs their "love," respect, and beneficence in order to secure his identity, visibility, survival and enhance his quality of life; and/or where he fears being overrun by overwhelming anxiety and personality disorganization should he lose their favor.

Under "normal circumstances" the targeted subject may enthusiastically, or through resignation or ignorance, accept and internalize the attitudes, etc., of his authority figures because of his genuine respect and love for them.

As the result of incorporating his authority figures' attitudes, etc., and successfully imitating or enhancing their behavioral characteristics, the subject may come to attain relatively high positive, though unauthentic, self-regard and "voluntarily" accept his assigned or achieved role in society. However, under "less normal" or "abnormal" circumstances the targeted subject ambivalently accepts and incorporates the attitudes as represented by his authority figures. That is, he accepts them tentatively, with severe reservations, resentment, contempt, and with intent to rebel against them. This may happen because he dislikes, fears, and/or may even detest the authority figures who represent them, dislike the ways they treat or relate to him, resent his dependence on them and yet must ostensibly obey their strictures in order to avoid punishment by them, and because he has learned or perceives no socially acceptable alternative ways of behaving. His ambivalence includes both a need for dependence (respect, love, caring, sympathy, etc.,) and a need for independence (fear and/or rejection of dependence, authority, caring, sympathy, etc.).

Without socially acceptable alternatives or an effective countervailing system of values, attitudes and supporting network of social relations, however, such ambivalence may lead to conflicting or mutually nullifying motives, values and behaviors which may in turn result in apathy, indecisiveness, low frustration tolerance, lack of persistence and focus, a sense of meaningless and purposelessness, boredom and a related craving for excitement. Impulsiveness may result from an inability to discover any good reason to resist excitements of any kind.

The Black-on-Black criminal is one who unwittingly internalizes White racist attitudes, identifies them as his own and who accordingly acts them out. Possessed by unconscious self-contempt, contempt for other African Americans (as a result of his having internalized White racist attitudes and behaviors toward himself and his people) with which he is inextricably identified, and resentful of society as represented by White Americans and their submissive "nigger Toms," he becomes as it were, "a rebel without a cause." Driven by his unconscious internalization of White racist attitudes and behaviors, or his deluded acceptance of their seeming correctness, he relinquishes control over his temper, moral judgments, and sense of proportions. He becomes the plaything of his impulses, raw emotions and desires. He feels compelled to perform acts the reasons for which he can only offer "lame" or transparent rationalizations, or for which he can offer no explanation except to say: "I just *did* it — I don't know why." "I don't mean to do it. It just happens."

Ego Defense Mechanisms

Denial and distortion are the classical categorical means, commonly referred to as ego defense mechanisms, by which an ego complex avoids unpleasant confrontations with reality, itself, and its own pathological history and current functioning. Through denial and distortion of reality and its concomitant self-deception, the collective White American ego complex rationalizes and repressively ignores its origination and sustenance by means of its enslavement, rape, robbery, and murder of captive peoples; its ruthless, unconscionable, wasteful and toxic exploitation of the land, labor, and resources of other peoples; its unwarranted wars against other nations and cultures, its exploitative instigation of wars among them; its duplicitous diplomacy and propaganda, treachery and deceit, warmongering and incitations to riot; its colonizing, neo-colonizing, terrorizing, starvation, benign and malicious neglect, usurious taxation of captive populations; its segregations, discriminations, dehumanizations, psycho-manipulations of other peoples and nations in flagrant violation of its own vaunted moral preachments; its closing of its ears to the cries of its victims; the sclerotic hardening of its psychic arteries.

By means of defensive denial and distortion, self-deception and reversal of reality, the collective Eurocentric ego complex seeks to resolve its self-created conflicts and contradictions, to avoid feelings of guilt, shame and anxiety, to neutralize negative self-perceptions, and to protect its material advantages. To these ends its victims must be blamed for their own victimization. Their suffering must be seen as reflections of their own inherent deficiencies, of their servile *manifest destiny*, and of their being short-changed by God and Fate.

Societal amnesia, a society's repression of the memory of the traumatic experiences which created its structure and character, is markedly typical of the collective White American ego complex. The domination of African Americans is made all the more effective and comforting to the collective White American ego if its historical and current dominative processes are kept from its own consciousness and the consciousness of the subordinate African American community. Historically embarrassing behavior, lowly and criminal origins, revelations of social iniquities and their current progeny, hidden from consciousness, permit the myth of the inherent moral, social, cultural, intellectual superiority of the White American complex to persist unchallenged, and enhances the efficiency of its exploitation of Africans at home and abroad.

Ego defense mechanisms are essentially contradictions, whether by denial, or distortion, of reality. But in the context of vast power differentials such as between parent and child, or more relevantly, between White America and Black America, these mechanisms additionally become instruments of creation. The collective personality of the African American community is to a significant extent a product of the processes of White American collective ego defensive efforts. The collective African American personality thus partially represents the incarnation of a host of collective White American ego contradictions, which are manifested as African American intra-communal, inter-personal, intra-personal conflicts and maladaptive social relations. It is out of the conflicts between conscious goals, apparently benign behavior and unconscious perfidious drives and needs, in the collective White psyche which when denied and distorted in order to defend its collective self-image, that the Black victim is born to be blamed, punished and to self-destruct. Black-on-Black crime and violence are only two of the means by which Black self-destruction becomes a form of Black American genocide by proxy.

Projection

The personal ego, in order to protect itself against what it may perceive as overwhelming shame, guilt, and anxiety, from loss of face and material advantage as the result of confronting the reality of its history and inauthenticity of its current existence, may engage in various forms of self-deception, referred to as *defense mechanisms*. These mechanisms of egoistical self-protection and need-gratification can be divided into two broad categories: (1) *denial;* and (2) *distortion*. The first involves the exclusion from consciousness of painful and self-condemnatory memories, impulses, conflicts and contradictions, and certain perceptions of current reality. The second involves the self-serving misperception and misinterpretation of personal and interpersonal historical relations, personal thoughts and feelings, current and ongoing interpersonal relations and other aspects of reality. These broad categories of defense, which include some fourteen or more subcategories, are principally utilized by the personal ego in order to minimize, if not neutralize, the importance and impact of painful perceptions, as well as to avoid taking responsibility for correcting its psychopathology.

One of the most important means by which the personal ego defends itself against anxiety, very painful, unflattering though authentic self-perceptions, and protectively retains and perhaps enhances its hard-won privileges and prerogatives (secondary gains), is through activation of a subcategory of defensive denial referred to as *projection*. The standard textbook definition of ego defensive projection refers to it as the means by which the ego disavows or refuses to recognize its own discreditable traits and self-incriminating motives by attributing those traits and motives to others. The unwarranted attribution of its own negative characteristics and intentions to another not only serves to protect the ego's flattering self-perception, but also justifies its often negative attitudes toward, and hostile relations with, others. In this instance, perpetrator becomes victim or intended victim, and victim becomes perpetrator. A reverse psychology is achieved. The projecting ego's false self-concept and misbegotten prerogatives are conserved. Projection provides a means by which the ego can simultaneously express and disclaim its self-incriminating impulses.

Textbooks aside, we must recognize that defensive projection is a way of life, a way of being and moving in the world. Projection does not only require an attributing to, or projecting of the ego's self-incriminating characteristics on the other, but a transformation of internal, potentially disorganizing contradictions into externalized attributive images and tensions; images and tensions which serve to structurally maintain the functionally dynamic organization of the ego. To project threat is to see it reflected in the face of the projective target or person. This self-instigated reflection creates a reactive psychological experience in the projecting ego. The ego projects threats and is threatened by its own reflected projection. Yet it denies or is unaware of its projective participation and creation of the threat it perceives, and believes it to be radiating independently from the other.

Through projection, the White American community transfers or exports its external contradictions — the conflicts, self-incriminations and tensions they engender — from itself to the African American community. By this means it rids itself of certain discomforts and discontents by forcing them on the Black community and perceiving them as originating in that community. By so doing it can better deny those characteristics in itself.

The same characteristics which when they are endemic to the White community and are perceived as threatening to its equilibrium, integrity and functionality, are externalized onto the Black community through projection. Consequently, the threats that come from inside the White community are perceived as coming from the outside Black community and are therefore perceived as generated by the latter. Thus the White community makes it appear that it is threatened by a menacing Black community; an evil, criminal, Black community which jeopardizes its existence: not the evil criminal inclinations it contains within its own bosom. By compulsively defending itself against the projected "threat" the Black community represents, the White community *defends* itself against its own self-generated, but self-denied, threats. The White community thereby becomes blind to its own negative characteristics and the positive characteristics of its scapegoat, the Black community.

Through projection the White community seeks to transform its evil, criminal, genocidal characteristics and intentions into good, law-abiding characteristics and intentions. Thus its evil becomes good. Once it projectively criminalizes the Black community it feels free to treat it criminally. Thus, to defend its own positive self-perception against knowledge of its own criminality, the White community must falsely accuse the Black community of criminality. For the sake of its own positive self-perception, the White community needs to perceive the Black community as criminal, whether or not such is the case.

When the projecting party or projectionist has superior influential advantages, as in the case of the White community relative to the Black community, projection becomes introjection, an act of creation, of transforming and conditioning reality. *Introjection* refers to the process by which the individual incorporates and accepts the prohibitions, values, attitudes, and commands of others as his own even when their acceptance and incorporation may work against his objective interests. In addition to its usual meaning, introjection as used herein refers to the process by which a more powerful party through various means, "forces" a weaker party to accept or behave in accordance with his projected values, attitudes and such. When the projectionist is the more powerful, the chief reinforcer and punisher, his projection becomes not only an instrument of ego-defensive self-deception, but also an instrument for provoking self-deception in the other, the target of his projections. The distorted reality and falsified consciousness of the projective target, through introjection, becomes the reality distortion and falsification of the consciousness of the projecting party.

The projective relations between the relatively powerful White community and relatively powerless Black community constitute an authentic process of transformational social interaction. The dominant White community, by controlling the rhythm of Black community life, controls to a significant extent the setting and experience of Black people, their self-perception and perception of reality. The dominant White community, by means of projection, acts in ways that organize the motivational systems of the Black community so that those systems are a functional reflection of the White community's psychopolitical needs. *Introjective projection* onto the African community occurs when that community accepts and internalizes the stereotypical characterization of itself as projected by another.

Introjective projection is accomplished when through its manipulative use of reward and punishment, control of information, definition of reality, etc., the White community inculcates in the collective personality of that community, a complementary and supportive set of values, norms, and patterns of behavior. Through the projective activities of the White community the collective character of the Black community is effectively deformed, defiled, and motivated to concretely demonstrate the characteristics stereotypically ascribed to it. By these and other means, the pathology in the White community becomes infectiously represented in the Black community.

The White American and the worldwide European ruling classes in general, refuse to accept and repent of their historical and contemporary theft of the lands, resources, and taking of the lives of their own and other peoples; their enslavement, serfdom and peonage of their own and African peoples; their colonization and rapacious exploitation of virtually all non-White peoples; their eradication of whole ethnocultural groups; their mass murder of millions of persons; their scandalization and assassination of the character of African peoples; their destruction of many of the Earth's streams, rivers, lakes, seas and oceans (ecocide); the raping and wasting of its natural treasures; their loosening of incurable diseases on vulnerable populations; their development and use of weapons of mass destruction; their assassination of national leaders, overthrow of duly elected governments and other intrigues against legitimate organizations; their warmongering and dissemination of murderous arms among nations for profit and political advantage; their addicting of whole populations to self-destructive habits, appetites and drugs; their falsification of the consciousness of the Earth's peoples, and numerous other heinous crimes against Man and Nature.

Because of their need to deny their long criminal history and contemporaneous criminality, their refusal to recognize that they pose the gravest danger to every type of life on Earth, and their need to divert theirs and the world's attention away from the facts listed above, the White American and European communities must compulsively project the alleged criminal activities in the Black community as representing the greatest danger to American society and European civilization. This White American and European projective twist of reality is designed to have the world forget that when this world is cataclysmically destroyed, it will not be caused by drug dealers, petty thieves, muggers, Black-on-Black criminals, but will be executed by White, patriotic, highly educated and civilized scientists, law-abiding citizen soldiers, as well as cultured, well-mannered and well-behaved diplomats.

Projection is a way of seeing, of attending to the world, a way of apprehending and interpreting the world, of positioning oneself in relationship to others and the world. It is a way of being in the world which precludes seeing oneself, the other, and the world honestly and comprehensively. It precludes one from seeing himself for who he really is and from dealing honestly and justly with himself and others. Projection involves the creation of a "necessary fiction," a functional myth. It involves self-deception, distortion and denial of reality in service of supporting and maintaining ego identity, dominance and control of the self and of the environment.

Projection is the ultimate form of put-down. Through projection the projecting party demotes and degrades his projective target as he enhances his own self-perception and self-image. This maneuver permits the projecting party to think well of himself in spite of his unflattering character and morally reprehensible social behavior which may be self-destructive, as well as destructive of others. For the projecting party, reprehensible social behavior belongs always to the other. The threat always comes from the projectively degraded other. This leaves the projecting party with a puritanical sense of ethical superiority and innocence.

The Projecting Narcissist

When used to degrade the other and elevate himself, projection becomes an adjunct to the narcissistic strivings and pretensions of the projecting party. Narcissistic strivings may also be seen as the sources for projective activities. Through projectively degrading the other, the projective narcissist devalues the standards, opinions, and personal worth of others as he overvalues his own standards, opinions, and personal worth. The narcissist feels affection only for himself, and he expects the other to hold him in the same unearned high regard and self-esteem in which he holds himself. He expects others to cater to his every whim. Others are perceived by the projecting narcissist as having been specifically created to be his servants and are therefore perceived to have no higher purpose than to oblige his comfort and welfare. They are perceived by him to be the instruments of his pleasures or displeasures. His interests take precedence over those of the projectively degraded others and his mere desire for something serves as the justification for his taking unauthorized possession of it. His right to take what he desires from others without their consent, and his expectation that he deserves special consideration from others are presumed by the projecting narcissistic party to be inalienable — to be God-given. Self-assured, self-centered, self-satisfied; proud of his often overblown achievements; preoccupied by unrelenting drives to achieve unassailable intelligence and competence, power and prestige; to maintain favorably wide differences in status and material wealth, physical beauty and apparent moral superiority; the projecting narcissist insists on his right to exploit the projectively degraded others. He may not hesitate to use cunning, and if necessary, ruthless force, to overcome anyone who dares stand between him and what he desires.

Oblivious to the fact that his behavior is unwarranted and irrational, the projecting narcissist experiences nothing but contempt and revulsion for those who fail to "respect" him or his wishes, and who may dare dispute his presumed privileges. The world revolves around the projecting narcissist and he only has affection for those who, knowing their "place," appear to be honored by his exploitative relationship to them and who seem to glory in the attention he deigns to pay them. His "love,"paternal protection and fidelity are extended only to those projectively degraded others who are obeisant, solicitous, subservient and self-effacing. The independence, equal or superior intelligence, competence and power of others are taken as personal affronts and as threatening to his security, self-confidence, self-image and social standing as well as his control of events, and are therefore the targets of the projecting narcissist's preemptive attacks.

For the projecting narcissist, interpersonal relationships are hierarchical. One is either superior or inferior; dominated or subordinated. He suspends the *Golden Rule* — and exempts himself from sharing with others as equals. He takes himself to be "above" the laws, conventions, ethics, mutual responsibilities which modulate, regulate and make possible harmonious reciprocal relations between persons. He may even consider himself "above" Nature and its laws as well. Nature is an instrumentality of his will and not an entity with which a relationship of reciprocity and balance must be maintained. In fact, the projecting narcissist thrives on social and natural imbalance, especially when such imbalance is perceived as supportive of his status and power advantages. He perceives such imbalance as crucial to his self-esteem and sense of security. When he perceives himself as having the advantage, he exhibits an arrogant, snobbish disdain for, and indifference to, maintaining propriety of mutually beneficial social relations.

For the projecting narcissist there are few or no permanent and deep loyalties to social and cultural values, ethical principles, individuals and/or groups. His only substantive and abiding interest is in the fulfillment of his personal interests and desires. His flagrant disregard for the humanity and human rights of his projective target is rarely attended by conscious feelings of remorse or guilt.

Under more maliciously psychopathological circumstances, the projecting narcissist peremptorily behaves in ways to defensively ward off the fancied hostility and contempt, humiliating intentions and behavior of others. The defensive reactions of others to his often unprovoked and unwarranted attacks are utilized by the projecting narcissist to rationalize and justify his initial and subsequent negative behavior towards them. Because he has "painted" his projective target with his own stereotypical image, read his own repressed motivations into the activities of the other, and if powerful enough, introjected or injected his values and behavioral orientations into the personality of his projective target, the projecting narcissist believes himself to be omniscient. He fancies himself as knowing the character and intentions of his projective target better then the latter knows himself. Therefore he needs no tangible evidence or proof of his projective target's guilt or hostile intentions. He can safely ignore evidence and telling arguments against his suspicions or stereotypical perceptions of others. If his projective target is actually not guilty of the crime or conspiracy of which he is accused by the projecting narcissist, he is still considered to be guilty of some yet-to be-discovered crime (the "fact" that his crime is undetected is considered indicative of just how slick the culprit is) and is therefore still deserving of punishment. If the narcissist's projective target has not yet committed a crime or contemplated its commission, the projecting narcissist assumes that he is surely going to do so in the future. Therefore, preventive detention or some cautionary punishment is still in order. For the projecting narcissist the projective target is born of sin, born in sin, and born to sin. He is guilty of being alive!

To reiterate, projection reflects a psychological need of the projectionist to ignore, deny, or rationalize certain of his own socially and/or personally undesirable personality/behavioral characteristics, motivations and intentions by thus attributing them to others. He may further assert that these defensively attributed characteristics, behavioral and motivational orientations, are not only endemically possessed by his projective target, but are utilized by the latter to mount hostile attacks against him. This assertion may be used by the projectionist to rationalize preemptive, ostensibly defensive, preventative, or retaliatory attacks against his projective target. Through this psychological maneuver, the attention of the projectionist and others are directed away from his faults and sly machinations and onto the alleged character, the hostile intentions and injurious behavior of the projective target.

Often the additional focus and much of the psychological resources and potential of the projective target himself may be diverted away from understanding the game to which he is subjected by his engaging in often vain attempts to defend himself against the projectionist's negative attributions. Under certain circumstances — these defensive attempts combined with powerful manipulations on the part of the projectionist — the projective target may come to actually acquire some characteristics the projectionist first falsely attributed to him. The projective target's attempts to compensatorily disprove the projectionist's stereotypical perception of him are often flattering to the projectionist's ego. They indicate the target's need for the projectionist's approval and attests to the projectionist's superiority. The projective target's need for the projectionist's approval, to buy his respect, is often used by the projectionist to his psychological and material advantage. Therefore, the more the projective target attempts to compensatorily gain the approval of the projectionist, the more he contributes to the power and status of the latter. The introjection of the projectionist's stereotypical expectations by the projective target, flatters the projectionist's sense of omnipotence, supports his denial of certain negative aspects of his own personality, embellishes his self-image, gives reason for his defensive dominance and disdain of the projective target. Thus, the projectionist profits from the projective target's reactionary responses to his stereotypical impositions, be they socially acceptable or reprehensible. The projective target is damned either way by the projectionist. The projectionist instigates, maintains, and is flattered by his target's neediness yet disparages him for his dependency and weakness.

The projecting narcissist loves to hate his projective target. It is a hatred that makes him feel good, righteous and justified.

Narcissistic Racism

When the projecting narcissist of one race makes his projective target the member of another race, the essence of racism is achieved. Projection, when combined with racial narcissism where a wide power differential in racial power exists, can be the source of a broad spectrum of psychological disturbances in the personal and social relations of the projective target. Malevolent narcissistic projection is the means by which the psychopathology of the racist projectionist is transferred in an unconsciously collusive and complementary way to his projective target.

It is through the use of malevolent narcissistic projection and other adjunctive psychological, "other-offensive" and self-defensive mechanisms, conjoined with supporting attitudes and behaviors, that the psychopathology of White American racism is transferred to the Black American community. Once transferred, it takes possession of the collective African American psyche and by distorting its self-perception, self-knowledge and reality-perception, transforms it into a psychological supporting actor whose role is to aid the White American community in maintaining its oppression. Thus it acquires its capacity for self-destruction. The relationship between the White American and the African American community is that of *folie 'a deux,* — a shared psychosis; a form of psychopathological "contagion" in which the Black American community inversely, and against its own interests, internalizes and incorporates into its own collective personality structure the racist delusions and other psychotic patterns of the White American community.

The "Law-abiding" White Community

As implied by the previous discussion, the White American community projectively degrades the African American community in order to support its pretentiously positive and narcissistic self-image, as well as to maintain its material and psychological advantages. As is the case with the projecting narcissist, the White American community devalues the worth and humanity of the Black American community as it overvalues its own worth and humanity. Through religious propaganda, falsification of history, the misreading and misinterpretation of its economic, cultural, technological, and military achievements, the White community has suffused its collective psyche and personality with narcissistic delusions of grandeur. Believing its own religious and racist propaganda, the White community perceives itself to be a *chosen people*: a people whose *Manifest Destiny* is to rule over other peoples. It perceives itself as on the top of a cosmically designed racial color pyramid apexed by blond Aryan races, and founded on the wooly-haired black African races. In the American societal context, the White American community imported Africans to serve as *its* bonded servants and continues to see the African American community as playing an *updated* version of Black servitude. The latter community is perceived as a lower form of humanity to which the ethical, moral, legal, personal considerations, and rules of etiquette (which expectedly inhere among members of the White community) need not apply.

The White community's narcissistic projection permits it to deny that its relationship to, and treatment of, the African American community is racist and criminal, and that its criminal treatment of the Black community is to a significant extent responsible for the alleged criminality and other forms of maladaptive behavior extant in that community. Furthermore, the narcissistic self-perception of the White American community and its obsessive negative stereotyping of the African American community, permits it to be relatively "law-abiding," considerate, civil, ethical and mutually self-respecting within its own communal boundaries while not exercising the same relative to the African American community. Believing the African American community to be deserving of its contempt, believing that its exploitation of that community is not criminal but an exercise of its God-given prerogatives, the White American community perceives no contradiction in engaging in, and condoning the kind of behavior within the African American community which it condemns as criminal, and which is punitively prohibited within its own provinces. Being a law onto itself and perceiving itself and its kind as penultimately humane and civilized, the White American community narcissistically expects and demands that those it degrades, disrespects, exploits, and grievously injures in innumerable ways, treat it with respect and even affection. It chooses to define its character in terms of intra-communal relations and not in terms of its regrettable extra-communal relations, especially with the Black community. Law-abiding and honorable in its own eyes, it permits itself to perceive itself as undeservedly victimized when reactionarily assaulted or offended by its victims. Honor, in the White community, is an "honor among thieves."

Narcissistic White Racism: A Model for the Black-on-Black Violent Criminal

The egocentrism of the malevolent projecting narcissist blinds him to the nature of his misperception and the related mistreatment of his projective target. It also blinds him to the fact that his mistreatment of his projective target serves to shape the latter according to the narcissist's stereotypical image of him. Moreover, the malevolent projecting narcissist's abusive relationship with his projective target serves as an inadvertent behavioral/attitudinal model for his projective target of how to deal with stress, frustration, and need-satisfaction. Additionally, the projecting narcissist's mistreatment of his projective target directly and indirectly communicates a set of judgmental attitudes toward his target which may then be internalized by the latter, and transformed by him into a set of negative self-concepts and behavioral directives: directives which may cause the projective target in turn to mistreat those who possess less power than himself the way he was/is mistreated by his more powerful projecting narcissist overlord.

> Indeed, research conducted within the framework of social-learning theory...demonstrates that virtually all learning phenomena resulting from direct experiences can occur on a vicarious basis through observation of another person's behavior and its consequences for them. Thus, for example, one can acquire intricate response patterns merely by observing the performances of appropriate models; emotional responses can be conditioned observationally by witnessing the affective reactions of others undergoing painful or pleasurable experiences; fearful and avoidant behavior can be extinguished vicariously through observation modelled approach behavior toward feared objects without any adverse consequences accruing to the performer; inhibitions can be induced by witnessing the

behavior of others punished; and finally, the expression of well-learned responses can be enhanced and socially regulated through the actions of influential models. Modeling procedures are, therefore, ideally suited for effecting diverse outcomes including...transmission of self-regulating systems, and social facilitation of behavioral patterns on a group-wide scale.[15]

With its narcissistic self-image gained by self-deceptive projections of its criminal motivations, intentionalities, and criminal character onto the African American community, the White American community is unable to acknowledge and come to terms with its own criminal history and contemporary crimogenic behavior toward the African American community. Furthermore, by projectively ignoring its deliberate stereotypical degradation, abuse, and exploitative treatment of the African community while narcissistically misrepresenting itself as the apotheosis of beauty, refinement, humanity, genius, civility; of responsible temporal power, prestige, and of moral superiority — the White American community chooses not to realize that it serves as the perfect model for the narcissistic Black-on-Black criminal. The contradictions the White American community as the premier behavioral/attitudinal model in American society represent are primarily responsible for spawning all the various gradations of criminality and other forms of personal and subcultural maladjustments that characterize both the White American and Black American communities today.

The White narcissistic racist as a model shares many of the following characteristics with the Black-on-Black criminal:

- Self-centered — he perceives his need satisfaction as more important than anything or anyone else's.
- His desire for something is reason enough for attaining it by any means necessary.
- Sociopathic, he maintains few or no permanent and substantial loyalties to any moral codes, persons, or group.
- He has a talent for rationalizing his criminal behavior so that it appears to himself and others that it is warranted, reasonable, and justified.

---

[15] Bandura, Albert. *Principles of Behavior Modification.* N.Y.: Holt, Rinehart and Winston, Inc., 1969.

- Frequently callous, impulsive or insidiously compulsive, aggressive and driven by an intense craving for excitement, he experiences little if any guilt and remorse after committing the most reprehensible acts.
- A social Darwinist, he believes in the philosophy of the "survival of the fittest" and acts as if the common courtesies, established conventions, and mutually supportive behavior does not apply to him.
- Often socially arrogant and rebellious, he perceives others as less human and less deserving than himself; as objects for exploitation, self-gratification, self-aggrandizement, and enhancing his self-esteem.
- Exhibiting a deep need for self-assurance and security he seeks to achieve and maintain absolute control of his environment. He therefore perceives any opposition to his goals as an insult to his dignity. He may sadistically gain pleasure in intimidating and assaulting others and overrunning his opposition with cold-blooded ruthlessness.
- Characterized by a self-deceptive sense of omnipotence, superiority and self-confidence, he finds pleasure and self-definition in conquest: conquest is its own justification.
- While he may be highly intelligent, facile and competent, he manifests little self-knowledge, foresight, or self-insight, and appears markedly unable, despite ample intellectual potential, to understand the full implications of his attitudes and behavior. In fact, his intellectual energies are almost completely devoted to fully developing exploitative techniques and technologies, cunning lies and clever machinations: tools for unjustly taking from others what he believes to be his due.
- Driven by a need to assert and prove his superiority, afraid of dependence, fearful and mistrustful of others, he aggressively strives for independence and places his faith only in himself and his ability to remain independent of those who may injure and humiliate him. For him "might makes right."
- Fundamentally a coward and a bully, he is motivated by an unrecognized inferiority complex. Highly sensitive to what he perceives as insults and put-downs or challenges to his "manhood," he intensely desires and often demands that others give him undeserved "respect."

- Afraid of betrayal, distrustful of love, deep feelings and attachments he experiences life as essentially meaningless and empty. He views the goodness of others as phony, as a cover for weakness and guile, as hypocritical and ineffectual, and as "asking to be used or taken advantage of." He is expert at pointing out the duplicity of others.
- Basically immature, he treats what he perceives as weakness and a lack of manliness in others with contempt.
- To successfully violate laughably pretentious institutional roles and regulations, to vandalize staid institutional establishments, to breach their forfeited walls and ransack their treasuries, to intimidate their human representatives and clients, evokes in him an ecstatic sense of God-like power: assuaging a basic and unrecognized sense of powerlessness and nothingness.
- Devoid of effective moral values, long-term commitments and preeminent goals, cultural and group identity; under the unrestrained pressure of his acquired needs, he is quintessentially motivated by the pleasure principle.
- For him, his intended victims have no rights they cannot defend successfully against his depredations. His victims' hapless or feeble resistance to being overrun by his well-executed blitzkrieg is a source of his personal sense of power, vengeance and triumph.
- An authority onto himself, he is the legitimizer of his own behavior. His victims have rights only he may condescendingly give them.
- A fatalistically self-serving and cunning rationalizer, he reasons that his victims get "what they have coming to them"; that they get what they deserve. "If he got it he deserved it." "If he had not gotten in the way he would not have been hurt." "It's his fault." "If he was supposed to keep what he had then I would not have been able to take it from him." He believes you should "never give a sucker an even break." His victim always "asks for it."
- He fears beyond Hell itself, the invisibility, nothingness, numbness, nobodiness, and alienation that "law-abiding" life and special custom seem to offer him. It is against this image of life that he rebels. He is not to be ignored. Somehow he must be noted, even if notorious.

- He equates violence with masculinity. His capacity for violence is correlated with his sense of security, his use of it, the most appropriate expression of his "manhood." Violence is often his most effective way of gaining "respect," control of others, and his environment.

A close examination of the above list should reveal that the Black-on-Black violent criminal in American society is essentially a "copycat," or imitator of the narcissistic racism endemic to the White American community. The Black-on-Black criminal, like the White narcissistic racist he imitates, does not find it difficult to violate the Human and Civil rights of others, to abuse the dignity, or to violently assault and murder others with impunity; feels free to dispossess others of their wealth and resources; perceives others as less human and less deserving of respect than himself; of being unworthy of being treated as he himself wishes to be treated. He does not honor the history, culture, pride and humanity of other people but rather seeks them out as special targets of degradation. He is the paragon of White racism in Black face. The Black-on-Black criminal is the *supreme* White racist and White supremacist.

The narcissist, even if he can love only what he perceives to be himself, can only love a fantasy. For the self he loves so obsessively, so exclusively, is for the most part, a hallucination, or at best, an amplified, anxiety-based embellished illusion of the self he actually is. He is in love with a half-truth or a lie. He loves and admires himself for values and attributes he either does not possess, or possesses in significantly less quantity and quality than he claims. Moreover, he expects others to love and admire him for the attributes and values he so conspicuously displays. Thus, the narcissist lives in a state of significant self-deception and demands that others affirm him in that state. If he succeeds in attaining the admiration, self-definition, and positive self-regard he craves, then he succeeds in gaining the "joys" their attainment bring based on self-deception and the deception of others. He therefore has a vitally personal interest in maintaining and living in a distorted and illusive world. Any threats to belie his world evokes severe anxieties and insecurities to which he reacts defensively, and in the case of the Black-on-Black violent criminal, offensively.

The Black-on-Black violent criminal is one who, like the rest of his victimized brothers and sisters, has been spooked by alienating demands of White American/European domination. The distortions of reality the fulfillment of these demands require, have been and are such that many oppressed Blacks feel compelled, for the sake of survival and peace, to adopt unrealistic standards of weights and measures in regard to themselves, the world, and reality. As a person who lives in captivity, who is supposed to serve at the pleasure of others, he possesses no rights of his own, or rights Whites are compelled to respect. He supposedly lives for the sake of his White captors as opposed to his own people. As such, he is loved and hated for the imagined qualities he does or does not possess relative to the needs of his White oppressors, rather than those other qualities he may indeed possess.

Under such circumstances the Black narcissist comes to love or hate himself in terms of what he imagines himself to be. The confrontation of the narcissistic, Black-on-Black, violent criminal with his oppressed reality is such that he feels that he can only be loved or protected for his imaginary qualities, for a falsely projected self, rather than his real self. Self-alienated, disconnected from his real self, he is also disconnected, does not know and therefore cannot be guided by his own volition, his own feelings, needs, likes and dislikes. He cannot appraise and truly know the dimensions nor evaluate the values of the self which he has not been permitted, or is afraid, to perceive. His self-esteem and self-estimation therefore become overly sensitive to the opinions of outsiders. Their high estimations of who he is, are desperately and obsessively sought and cultivated.

Fantasies of the Black Narcissistic Criminal

The self-inflated fantasies of the Black narcissistic criminal are the sources of substitute counterfeit satisfactions. Though his self-inflated fantasies and illusions are by definition not real, the satisfactions he garners therefrom, though only partially gratifying, are. For him these satisfactions such as they are, are better than nothing; better than sinking into abject compliance or despair. If his acted-out fantasies are the source of positive self-feelings, self-regard and peer acceptance, if they bring some otherwise unavailable material satisfactions, then for him they

are real and worth defending with his life — and worth sacrificing the lives of others. Through his acted-out fantasies the Black-
on-Black criminal experiences a triumph, a sort of "get over,"
a sort of "get back" on the "Man" and his system — a system
designed to kill him spiritually, if not physically.

But the violent Black-on-Black narcissistic criminal in his
triumph reveals his self-contempt, cowardliness, and contempt
for his people. His violent narcissism reveals that he cannot
believe his real self to be truly lovable. He substitutes for genuine
love, admiration and respect, the love, admiration and respect
of others gained under false pretenses. Deep inside he knows
that he is a fake. Deep inside he hates himself for what he has
become. Despite his apparent "getting over" on the system, he
has surrendered to it in a devious fashion. He is not the hero
he makes himself out to be. His hostile, intemperate, and often
violent encounters with the world derivatively reveal his
inarticulate and misdirected self-contempt.

Self-Contempt, Self-Concept, Love and Violence

The Black-on-Black violent criminal hates in other Blacks those
characteristics he hates most in himself. His expressed contempt
for and attacks on other Blacks are the means by which he
refrains from recognizing and expressing his self-contempt. By
externalizing his self-contempt he stays his own hand from
attacking himself. He commits *homicide* to keep from committing
suicide. His homicidal mania, violent rages, are curious and
perverted forms of self-preservation.

> He is compelled, therefore, to externalize his self-contempt, to
> blame, berate, humiliate others. This, however, throws him in
> the toil of a vicious circle. The more he despises others the less
> he is aware of his self-contempt — and the self-contempt grows
> more violent and merciless and the more hopeless he becomes.
> To strike out against others is then a matter of self-preserva-
> tion.[16]

Yet the narcissism of the violent Black-on-Black criminal
denotes a strange, dangerous sort of neurotic pride which does

---

[16] Horney, K. *Our Inner Conflicts: A Constructive Theory of Neurosis.* New York:
Norton, 1966.

not permit him to admit consciously and exhibit publicly his utter humiliation and captivity. He fashions, in self-destructive ways and in ways destructive to others, power out of powerlessness; triumph out of defeat. He throws the hate and contempt thrown on him onto others and seeks to obtain sustenance thereby. Like his narcissistic White oppressor counterpart, he lives off his hatred and contempt, his violent, exploitative, cunning use and abuse of Black people. He gleefully joins the White draculas as they suck the blood of their Black victims and cannibalize Black bodies in order to add to their powers and pleasures.

Genuine and unexploitative love is not possible under the regime of narcissism. The love and respect others demonstrate for the narcissist guarantees the evocation of his self-contempt for them. For if the people who love and respect the phony image he projects, he seriously doubts that they could love and respect what he unconsciously perceives himself to actually be. This doubt is the more intense the more his projected narcissistic image deviates from his hated actual self. Others playing along with his narcissistic charade makes him doubt the genuineness of their love and respect, makes him see them as hypocritical. He knows they are suckers. By loving and respecting his phony presentation of himself his admirers unknowingly, and perhaps for narcissistic reasons of their own, imprison him within a dungeon of his own making. For this he hates them. For the reason he needs their phony admiration more than he needs to be honest and true to himself: he hates himself. Consequently, when he gives overt expression to these two hates he is compelled to act destructively as well as self-destructively.

The narcissistic Black-on-Black violent criminal seethes with self-contempt, envy, resentment, and vindictiveness. Though he dares not acknowledge it to himself, he has given up on making something of himself based on the presentation of his real self to the world. He hates himself for having given in to the pressure of others. He harbors a vindictive rage against others who pressured him to give in. He resents his having to pursue his phony existence while his oppressors seemingly are free to pursue their "real" interests. He envies them their freedom, their "enjoyment of themselves," their enjoyment of their material and social bounty.

He accepts the nihilistic dictum that none shall have joy, pleasure, happiness and material advantages if he has none. If good health, wealth, and happiness are denied him, why should others less deserving than he be permitted their enjoyment? Why should he be the only one left out?

Having accepted the notion promulgated by his White oppressors — that he will never measure up to their (projected as universal) standards, never be as "good" as they — he vindictively asserts that they will never be as "bad" as he. Thus, he finds near erotic delight in demonstrating himself to be the "baddest" who ever walked on earth. In this game he has a better than sporting chance to win. In this game he makes the rules.

The essence of the Black-on-Black criminal is self-hatred or self-alienation. These can only be learned. Self-hatred can only occur as the result of the self having been made to appear to be hateful, ugly, degrading, rejected, associated with pain, nonexistent or devoid of meaning, and inherently inferior. Such appearances and associations are the fruits of White American narcissistic racist projections against the African American community.

As the controller of information, the "validator" of truth, minister of education and instruction, role model, chief reinforcer, as the *Final Word* and ultimate authority, it is the White American community that must bear the responsibility for injecting as the central motivating factor self-hatred, or more accurately, self-alienation, into the heart of the Black-on-Black criminal and the minds of the rest of the maladjusted African American community.

The Black-on-Black violent criminal is what he is because he has been treated criminally at some crucial points in his life, and/or treated to a history or a model of criminality. He is within a context that evokes criminal behavior not inhibited or redirected by effective opposing or alternative moral, intellectual, socioeconomic, cultural and valuational structures. The Black-on-Black criminal is violent because he has been violated, or perceives himself as such. He is vindictive. He wants to "pay the world back" for some insult he most often cannot name or define, an insult which may have resulted in his having been conceived and born; an insult which occurred to him in the womb; an insult for which he wishes to vindicate himself, for that which occurred centuries before he or his parents were born — a history of unrequited grievances.

Through his often unprovoked or excessive violence he wishes to childishly and magically undo the curse or dogged bad luck which has been imposed on him by others. His violent search for power, status, material worth, excesses and comforts, hostile independence, is energized by a thousand psychological nicks and cuts. His criminality springs from a deep well of hate and desire for retribution, vindication and a perverted, bellicose, bloodcurdling, self-defeating cry for love and understanding.

He is afraid of feeling, of being sensitive: for with these come pain and humiliating manipulations. Having buried feelings deep inside himself, yet needing to feel and be excited, to experience pleasure, to be "connected," he can only satisfy such needs and acquire such experiences by exposing himself to dangerous life-threatening situations. He makes others bend to his will, feel his pain and humiliation intensely. It thrills him to see their feelings writ large on their faces, on their trembling bodies as they fearfully emit unheralded cries for help and mercy. He is a man without empathy. How can a man empathize with something less than a man? How can one express what he has not discovered in himself and the world, or what he has not been taught or has learned how to express himself?

The Black-on-Black criminal is unforgiving. He is an Old Testament devotee: "An eye for an eye, and a tooth for a tooth!" He is the Lord and vengeance is his. He disdains social conventions because he is disdained by social conventions. He deceives as he is deceived. He does not respond to punishment because he believes that he is being punished for the crimes of others and because he and his kind have a long history of being unfairly accused. Having been the object of the hedonistic cravings of others he vindictively makes others the object of his hedonistic impulses. His feelings having been disregarded by others, he retaliates by disregarding the feelings of others. His insensitive treatment at the hands of those more powerful than himself provides him with a rationale for ignoring and treating others insensitively. Having himself been the object of others' sensual excitement and perverse pleasures, he finds a cruel satisfaction, excitement, and pleasure in intimidating, hurting, and degrading others. He denies his own downtroddeness by trampling down others — a victim who victimizes in order to assuage the pain of his own victimization.

The Black-on-Black criminal's imagination is heroic. His heroism is cut whole-cloth from the White heroes he imitated as a child and adolescent man: the ones he saw in the comics, cartoons, movies and read about in the newspapers...who were always White. He uses their lingo, their cars, exaggerates their dress, spends their kind of money, kills with their weapons and with their heartlessness. He is a cartoon playing itself out in real time — a man acting like "the man" (*White man*). When he acts, he acts with a White man's image in his head as a model: copying boyhood heroes and villains. Now, as then, he and the White hero he imagines himself to be are one. He can only see other Blacks as "Toms," pimps, cons and chumps: heroes never! As a hero in his own mind he is not one of them (chumps). He's different.

The Black-on-Black criminal's only problem is that he is not really "the man." He does not possess *the power* to legitimize his victimization of his race. And this is what makes him an outlaw — not his attitudes, not his violent behavior, his victimization of his brothers. These are the White man's prerogatives. His crime is exercising them "illegitimately."

A common belief held by most Americans, both Black and White, is one that holds that whether by pluck or luck, the "haves" are better than or superior to the "have-nots." The Black-on-Black violent criminal, suffering unrewarded pluck and down on his luck, builds on that logic. If he can "better" his betters, can triumph over their superiority, can confiscate their possessions, can make them quake and tremble for their "goody-goody" lives, is he not then the better, the superior, the more powerful man? All of this and the ecstatic sweetness of revenge, the joys of having, addicts him to his instrumental use of violence. He thinks he has found a way to outwit what he mistakenly believes to be his and his people's destiny.

He clownishly parades the spoils of his war against himself and his people as testaments to his majesty and bravery. He dares not face the fact that they are but the yellowed emblems of cowardice. They give a testimony of his given up or having fled in lily-livered fear the fighting of his oppressors to the death. He apparently cannot even accept as a reasonable possibility the dethronement of his oppressors. He has accepted defeat. His Black-on-Black violence attests to his loss of nerves, his loss of faith in himself, and in the idea that his patient, hard-won self-development can gain him the rewards he so desires and deserves based on his own terms, and not those of sneak thieves, dope peddlers, bullies, brutes, muggers, and murderers — the terms of the truly weak and wicked.

Why is the African American Community not totally Criminal?

At this point the question must arise which in effect asks: If, given its powerful influence, the narcissistic racism of the White American community provides a model of criminality for the African American community, and its intention toward and relationship with the latter community is so malevolent, why is there not a much higher rate of criminality among African Americans? Why is the African American community not a camp of thieves, a total criminal formation?

In answer, credit must be given to the moral resolve of African peoples, to the traditional moral attitudes and behaviors of African culture which were not totally denatured in the crucible of slavery, and the grossly negative experience of being African in America. More specifically, the images the White American community projects onto the African American community, the spirit it seeks to inject into the African American character is not monolithic or one-sided. White American narcissism is equivocal. When it projects its programmatic racial attitudes and images onto the African American community, it projects contradictions. White American projection *speaks with forked tongue* — talks out of *both sides of its mouth*. The dominant, powerful, exploitative White American community when engaged in projective self-defense, projects "good" as well as "evil." In fact it projects ambivalence into its projective object, the African American community. Its projective implant in the center of the collective African American psyche is both devil and angel, Dr. Jekyll and Mr. Hyde. At the same time the projecting White community thrusts its evil, stereotypical images and appraisals on the African American community, it projects moral/ethical concepts and preachments, and projectively represents itself and its hypocritical behavior as preeminent models of human goodness and moral acquittal.

Simultaneous with its moral exploitation of the African American community (and in support of it), the dominant White American community projects and injects its moral code directly and indirectly into the African American collective psyche. In fact, it presumes to give the African American community religious and moral instructions. These instructions along with their adjunctive blandishments and inducements come to constitute a large part of the ego-ideal or superego, or conscience of the latter community. It is under the influence of this White American moral introject that the subordinate African American community is expected to gain and exercise "moral self-control."

Both the moral codes and the negative stereotypes injected into the collective psyche of the African American community by the projecting White American community, are designed to protect and guard the interests of the latter community; to neutralize and attenuate any challenge to its hegemony by the former community. This implanted set of moral codes ensconced in the collective psyche of the African American community are obeyed or infracted in ways that justify and reinforce the power status quo between the two communities. Under the leverage of these codes the large majority of African Americans become "good," "decent," and "law-abiding": citizens abiding by laws made by others and to the advantage of the law-makers. These implanted codes function to inhibit justifiable revolutionary behavior on the part of the subordinate African American community. In the form of anticipatory guilt, the conscience implanted in the collective African psyche by the White American community inhibits any immoral "unlawful" thoughts and behavior on the part of the African community which threaten to rewrite the equation between the races.

The subordinate African American community which lives under the regime of its implanted, coercive White Christian conscience is chronically caught in a classic double-bind. That is, since the conscience or the superego implanted is an agent of the White American community's psychic and material exploitation of the African American community, both the latter's obedience to and/or defiance of the admonitions of its implanted moral arbiter become acts of self-negation, and in many instances, acts of self-destruction.

European Time and African Identity

To be an African living under European domination is to live in a time-warp, to live out of sync, and is therefore tantamount to living in a state of false consciousness. To know one's time is to know oneself. To know one's rhythm, and to live in accord with it, is to live harmoniously and healthily. To live by running against the grain on one's time, to live according to another's time, is to live anemically and maladaptively. It is to be enslaved by one's timekeeper — to live for him, and not for oneself. This is the African situation.

Having been removed against their will from their continent, the Africans have been denied access to their own self-generated time and rhythms: rhythms, the means by which time reveals itself to consciousness, rhythms that were the very evolutionary infrastructures of their minds, bodies, consciousness, social relations, social organizations, destinies and identities. More damaging than the capturing and domination of African bodies was the subversion and the fragmentation of African time.

Yet, the psychological dismembering and reconstruction of African time was and is necessary to the domination and exploitation of Africans by Europeans, whether as slaves, social outcasts, second-class citizens, honorary White men, highly paid servants, entertainers, gladiators, or as "low-lifes," criminals, mendicants, illiterates and "slow-learners," heedless hedonists, conspicuous consumers, poor or negative examples. In gaining control over the African sense of time, Europeans gained control over African consciousness and through this their behavioral orientations, power, and possibilities. In warping African time Europeans warped African identity and attempted to ensure their slavish dependence.

Who one is and what one is about, where one stands relative to others, is determined by one's sense of history, sense of the present, and the future, and the connectedness of all three. One's perceptions of his past, present and future, whether ordered linearly or non-linearly, form the space-time coordinates which define oneself. Those who control another's perceptions of his history, current reality and experience, and assume responsibility for his future, control his self-definition and limit his behavioral possibilities. Where these space-time coordinates become malleable, identity and related behavior become malleable as well.

European control of African space-time coordinates (i.e., the European control of the interpretation of the African past, present, and future) means European control of African identity and vision, the Eurocentric shaping of African identity and vision to suit their imperial needs.

Europeans in disconnecting, scandalizing, stealing and distorting African time, simultaneously fragment, neuroticize and psychopathologize the African personality. Any African bereft of his knowledge of true African history (and conversely, of true European history) is denuded of self-knowledge, self-acceptance, and self-love. He thereby fails to learn all the lessons and techniques his past can teach him: lessons, the learning of which are indispensable to his liberation. He loses his memory and power of the word, suffers amnesia, and feels he was only born when delivered and slapped on the behind by European midwifery. Consequently, he experiences and perceives himself as one who is yet undeveloped and dependent and in need of European care and nurturing. Life outside of European paternalistic domination becomes a fearful abstraction. He is only "real" when under the focused attention of his European paternalistic overseers. He does not desire the end of European domination, only the end of its mistreatment of him. He only wishes that it be benevolent, for he has been made to think that left to his own devices, to the reckoning of his own time he will be overtaken by darkness, chaos, and insanity, that his new world, absent of a European presence, will be peopled by demons and ghouls whose faces bear a remarkable resemblance to his own.

Having lost his own time, the captive African feels that his personality and his whole being can only be organized and energized within the context of the European space-time matrix, and that the world would be void and without form in the absence of European acts of creation. Consequently, for him only European things are "the real thing," "the real McCoy," "the genuine article;" only they possess real value. Only the acquisition of things European, of a European identity, and their moral mastication can pacify his infantile anxieties and appetites.

With loss of control and responsibility for his future to the Europeans, the captive African also loses his sense of self-determined purpose, loses his identity, and with it, his sense of initiative, industry, self-determined creativity, organization of intellect, proactive development of his personality, and empowering relations. Walled off from his past and future, locked into his present, the captive African remains the reactionary prisoner of Europeans. His identity, or the lack thereof, is a reactionary creation, whether it be a caricature of the European middle- and ruling-classes, an imitation of life of "ordinary," "law-abiding," "church-going," "God-fearing," "hard-working" White folks, or the pseudo-independent copycatting of Al Capone, "Scar face," or a thousand other White criminals, gangsters, and reprobates. His lack of identity permits him to easily become this season's living, walking clothes rack, meandering advertising sandwich board, animated jewelry display case, chauffeur driven by his own limousine, or a nondescript, faceless beggar, hebephrenic idiot, or peripatetic septic tank.

Until we reclaim our African Time
We, all of us Africans, are Prisoners
And not accurately discerning
the causes of our Incarceration
We are assumed by onlookers
and ourselves to be Criminals
You know, the World thinks that if you are
in prison you must have committed some Crime

Our Imprisonment indicts Us
We must break out
The Executioner approaches
Time is of the Essence

5

THE IDENTITY CRISIS OF THE
BLACK-ON-BLACK CRIMINAL

...Negroes also have been not too subtly defined by the White majority in America as Public Enemy Number One in the so-called "war against crime." To the extent this is true, their dominant contribution to our crime problem has been ensured. The conscious or unconscious tendency among middle class whites to equate Negroes with crime has given the latter a final shove into total degradation and alienation, providing a powerful nothing-to-lose incentive to criminal acts.

— EDWIN SCHUR
Our Criminal Society

FOR THE BLACK-ON-BLACK VIOLENT CRIMINAL, identification with the White supremacist aggressor community is never complete, nor is his dis-identification with the victimized African American community. The Black-on-Black criminal is a hybrid, a victimized aggressor — one motivated and rationalized by his perceived victimization. Like all Africans subject to aggressive European domination he is neither "Peter nor Paul." He is caught between the horns of an unresolvable dilemma. He can never be a White man in the truest sense of the term, and he unalterably refuses to be a Black man in the true sense of the term. Having internalized the Eurocentric definition of what it means to be African — all negative — as well as having observed the material losses, social ostracism, victimization, rejection, etc., that Europeans and others have applied to those who identify themselves as African, he scurries to the safety of ethnic ambiguity or self-alienation. What "in-between" identity is chosen by the "average" African American, i.e., how much and what aspects of the White American racist aggressor and the Black victim he chooses to meld into his ambivalent personal identity, depends on many factors.

We must note that the Black-on-Black criminal as well as the "average" African American suffer most fundamentally from a chronically painful identity crisis from which they seek to find relief and/or escape. Many pathways to, and forms of relief are chosen, some more self-destructive and antisocial than others, all neurotic: many vacillating from one extreme to the other. Therefore, the "average" African American is synthetic, a Frankenstein creation of the American Dilemma. His synthetic identity is suffused with ambivalence, and based on misconceptions. For it is forged from two major falsified and self-serving Eurocentric projections — a projectively inflated, confabulated, European image and a complementary deflated, scandalized, apparently and repulsively exposed African image. Consequently, the victimized African with no positive African identity, and his identification with the false image of the European, can only achieve alienation from reality no matter how "normal," "law-abiding," "abnormal,"or "criminal" he may appear to be.

The Black-on-Black violent criminal, in forging his personality chooses to identify with, for whatever reasons, the violent, victimizing aspects of his White American racist aggressor, and attempts to reject or escape from his eurocentrically falsified, victimized African American image. In so doing he paradoxically incarnates and fulfills the eurocentrically projected stereotype of himself as criminal. His identification with his White supremacist aggressor is partial because he, on some subconscious level of his being, recognizes his own victimization by the aggressor, and seeks to revenge or compensate for it. He therefore aggressively or through subterfuge rejects the moral, ethical values and preachments of his White supremacist aggressors. He recognizes they are designed not to be applied to their own behavior and attitudes toward him, but are designed to prevent his retaliation against them and to make his victimization and exploitation more efficient and trouble-free. The violent Black-on-Black criminal feels the common African American ambivalence more intensely than do noncriminal African Americans. He is most sensitive to it and therefore represses it more deeply. He dissociates or splits off the pain from the emotion and only feels the vague indefinable frustration, invisible restraining forces, the anger, the restlessness, agitation, irritation and moodiness; the boredom, sense of purposelessness and meaninglessness, the painful states of consciousness that cry out from alienation and for violent expression.

Thus, the violent Black-on-Black criminal in many instances, being neither Black nor White, is but an ambivalent empty shell of a man whose bottomlessness, vacuity, numbness, and lack of definition are the sources of his insatiable need to fashion an identity from current fads, eccentric dress and behavior. His voracious and rapacious greed, his need to consume conspicuously, to become a gluttonous devourer of things and people, reflects his ethnic hollowness. His need to intensify the painful feelings of others are emblematic of his need to feel something within himself, to have someone else know the pain he has so deeply buried within. He kills the other so as to share his own death of spirit, humanity and deadness with someone else. His need to define reality and himself outside the consensus of others reflects his unrealistic definition by others, and his attempts to define himself through violent intrusion into their reality. The partial or complete fulfillment of these needs brings about in him an overpowering sense of excitement, aliveness, power, sensuality, imperial authority and masculinity (which he often equates with the capacity to injure and destroy others). Though he transcends the restricted world that surrounds him, he also experiences, simultaneously, an unconscious sense of guilt and self-condemnation. He cannot escape his ambivalence. Since his antisocial acts are the only ones which he assumes permit him to experience the overwhelmingly "positive" feelings just described (even his material acquisitions are only instrumental to evoking desirable feelings), and since his nymphomaniacal emptiness rapidly consumes these feelings, his hunger too soon becomes more painfully insistent. To repress his unconscious feelings of guilt, isolation, alienation and self-condemnation that threaten to break through to consciousness, he becomes helplessly addicted to those intoxicating feelings and the violent, antisocial means by which they are ameliorated. Even if he does not "enjoy" his use of violence, the Black-on-Black violent criminal sees it as instrumental to attaining the feelings to which he is addicted. As such, violence is at least secondarily positively reinforcing.

Poverty and Crime

The reader should note that the foregoing discussion is not solely an intrapsychic, "blaming the victim" exposition. The author does not differentiate between "outside" and "inside" as far as human psychology is concerned, even though didactic and linguistic styles and limitations make it appear so. The human being, as are all things, is continuous with the rest of the universe. The environment, objects whether living or nonliving, human or nonhuman, concrete or abstract, intrude into the human psyche and body via the media of feelings. The psyche transduces the material, dynamic, and abstract world in terms of feelings. It is to these feelings that the mind, body, and personality respond, process, and feed forward into consciousness and the world.

The assertion that mediating values, perspectives, etc., and the feelings they help to produce motivate criminal behavior, should not be construed to imply that conditions such as "poverty" do not contribute to criminality to a substantial degree. Furthermore, it should not be construed to imply that attitudes, values, etc., need only be changed in order to change the criminal behavior of those who live in poverty without improving poverty conditions themselves. A condition and the experiential reactions it appears to evoke are derivative of the synthesization of the individual's perception of his "real" physical, behavioral, social environment and the organized experiences and the motivations he brings into that environment. Consequently, significant changes in one stimulates related changes in the other and vice versa.

Indeed, the conditions under which the individual lives may significantly affect those with whom he associates; the perspectives, attitudes and values he internalizes, provide or fail to provide the resources, opportunities and other amenities, the patterns of which determine whether or not he engages in criminal behavior. The conditions under which African Americans live have been deliberately instituted by White America in order to accomplish definite ends. Joel Kovel speaks to this when he states that:

> ...throughout our history, whites have created the institutions by which black people are forced to live, and which force them to live in a certain way, almost invariably so as to foster just that constellation of unworthy traits. From slavery itself to modern welfare systems, this has been the enduring pattern, reinforced in popular culture and education by a panoply of stereotypes along the same lines.
>
> The result of these cultural manipulations has been to ensure to the black person a preassigned degraded role, no matter where he turned.[17]

Poverty in the United States is a *crime* committed against the African American population. White racism, and other forms of discrimination against Africans, are designed to maintain African Americans in relative and absolute poverty. Poverty represents the deliberate, vicious robbery, exploitation, and extortion of the labor, wealth and resources of the African community by the European/White American community. Thus, if crime is "caused by poverty," then Black criminality is crime White criminality produced. If African American crime is the psychologically-morally mediated outcome of poverty, or more specifically, the outcome of the psychological-moral factors "within the individual," then it still remains the crime that European/White American crime produced. Psychological-moral values are learned social-political products. People are taught to be moral by direct instruction, observational learning, personal-familial-community-peer group relations and experience, and prevailing overall politicoeconomic conditions. All these factors are under the dominative and self-serving influence of the European/White American community. Thus, intimating that African American criminality is the result of moral depravity

---

[17] Kovel, J. *White Racism: A Psychohistory.* New York: Columbia University Press, 1984.

the European/White American community unwittingly incrimi-
nates itself and reveals its own criminality. To avoid acknowledgment and confrontation with the fact that the moral attitudes
and values are learned by the means just mentioned, and the
means are under their control, the White American community
must allege that the "moral depravity" of African Americans is
genetic in nature: that it is inherited within their genes. Thus,
it absolves itself of all responsibility. It is this type of absolution
that sets up a vicious criminal mill wherein the European/White
American community produces the criminality it attributes to
innate African American venality. This is the most devastating
of European/White American self-fulfilling prophecies.

Wealth and Crime

Wealth, the feelings and the associated ideas it evokes in some
individuals, may motivate criminal behavior. Crime is not the
monopoly of poor folks, nor is greed, alienation, and so on. We
should note that a person or group is seldom if ever exposed to
one environment exclusively, particularly in the United States.
Poverty-stricken people know of and have been exposed to wealth.
They are often keenly aware of the material and social benefits
derived from being wealthy. This knowledge and experience,
along with the internalization of cultural myths concerning rights
and opportunities to acquire wealth, in conjunction with other
ideas and feelings, interact with the current situation to
determine behaviors, some of which may be labeled criminal.
Discrepancies such as between what is and what could be, what
is and how it got to be the way it is, are contradictions which
may motivate criminal behavior as a "symptomatic compromise."
It may be more the exposure to wealth, to the wealthy via direct
and indirect experience (e.g., reading, advertisement, etc.), which
is the source of criminal behavior, more so than the exposure
to poverty. Perspective, values, socio-ecological context, personal
characteristics, and any other number of other transducers may
evoke criminal behavior.

    In fact, violence of all types including robbery, thievery,
extortion, murder, are the monopoly of the middle- and ruling-
classes. Their apparent *noncriminality* is mainly due to the fact
that they define what crime is, and define out of existence their
own crimes. Their criminal activities are delegated through their

police forces (*enforcers*), armed forces (*gangs*), bankers (*loan sharks*), sales persons and advertising agents (*con artists*), business men (*extortionists* making offers others *cannot refuse*), diplomats (*front men*), corporations (*rackets*), consortiums (*drug and other types of rings*), and numerous other euphemistically named organizations whose nefarious activities are whitewashed by deceptive terms and legitimized by their power. Their taking of property, wealth, dignity, and lives of others by force is called *war*; their major massacres, called World War I and World War II, the winning of which were sources of immense feelings of joy, pride, narcissistic self-congratulation, increased power, prestige, and wealth for the "victors." Through delegation, distancing, and subtle use of the word, the middle- and ruling-classes deceive themselves and others into thinking of them as *beautiful people*.

> I spent thirty-three years and four months in active service as a member of our country's most agile military force — the Marine Corps. I served in all commissioned ranks from a second lieutenant to major-general. And during that period I spent most of my time being a high-class muscleman for Big Business, for Wall Street, and for the bankers. In short, I was a racketeer for capitalism....
>
> Thus I helped make Mexico and especially Tampico safe for American oil interests in 1914. I helped make Haiti and Cuba a decent place for National City Bank boys to collect revenues in.... I helped purify Nicaragua for the international banking house of Brown Brothers in 1909-1912. I brought light to the Dominican Republic for American sugar interests in 1916. I helped make Honduras "right" for American fruit companies in 1903. In China in 1927 I helped see to it that Standard Oil went its way unmolested.
>
> During those years I had, as the boys in the back room would say, a swell racket. I was rewarded with honors, medals, promotion. Looking back on it, I feel I might have given Al Capone a few hints. The best *he* could do was to operate his racket in three city districts. We Marines operated on three continents.[18]

---

[18] Major General Smedley D. Butler in John M. Swomley, Jr., *American Empire, The Political Ethics of the Twentieth-Century Conquest.* New York: The Macmillan Co. 1970. p.150.

White Control of Black Transduction

Transduction refers to the process wherein one form of energy or information is converted or transformed by some type of mediation system into another form. Hence, through some brain or neuronal mediational processes, ideas, perceptions, feelings, environmental information, ...may be transformed into behavioral acts or a variety of other products and processes. Transduction via "mind-set" attitudes, expectations, desires, etc., transforms environmental information into other forms of thoughts, feelings, emotions, etc., which are then utilized by the "mind" to originate and regulate behavior.

Persons who possess operatively different sets of values, desires, attitudes, abilities, resources, goals, self-perceptions, etc., who find themselves in the "same objective environment (physically speaking) will experience that environment different-ly, and behave differently in response to it. Consequently, a number of behavioral outcomes may flow from two persons reacting to the "same" environment — they may experientially and behaviorally respond in the "same" way, or in different ways. Two "objectively" different environmental circumstances may produce the same experiential/ behavioral response in two persons due to the different orientations brought to them by those persons. Thus, greed may be evoked by wealth in some individuals while poverty evokes greed in others.

To a significant extent, sociopolitical power held by one person or a group of persons, permits that person or group to manipulate the valuational/perceptual attitudes of another less powerful person or group, and thereby manipulate their transductive experiences, and through these their behavioral output. White America by naming, defining, interpreting and abstracting the world, by associating various aspects of it with pleasure or pain, seeks to control and name the experience of Black America and thereby name and control its reactive and proactive behavior. Because this White American conspiracy which more often than not operates on a subliminal level is consciously perceived by the Black individual as his own transductive attitudes, feelings, perceptions, etc., they appear to him to be "logically," "naturally," "universally," "divinely," and therefore unquestionably real and true. He thinks that he alone is the determiner of his attitudinal/behavioral tendencies. Until

African Americans develop their own transducing or transforming values and identity (which is a system of values, precepts, etc.,) based on a thorough objective analysis of their historical, immediate, and anticipatory reality, they will be the unwitting pawns of European/White American self-serving needs and desires.

Neither Poverty nor Wealth alone
*   makes a man criminally avaricious*
In both cases his thievery is motivated by
*   his desire to own more than he already possesses*
And by his willingness to break the laws
*   in order to attain his heart's desires*

The type of crime a man tends to commit
*   is more a reflection of his social status*
*   values and opportunity*
Than it is a measure of his presumed Venality
*   Accountants embezzle*
Why mug someone when you can more easily and
*   profitably "cook the books"?*
The Lower classes rob Houses
*   The Ruling classes rob Nations*

In the area of Drug Rehabilitation
*   it should be the Pusher who is*
*   the object of Detoxification*
For it is his Addiction that is
*   the true cause of addiction in others —*
His Addiction to the American Dream

6

SELF-ALIENATION

Self-hate finally culminates in pure and direct *self-destruc-tive impulses and actions*. These may be acute or chronic, openly violent or insidious and slow grinding, conscious or unconscious, carried out in action or performed in imagination only. They may concern minor or major issues. They aim ultimately at physical, psychic, and spiritual self-destruction.

— KAREN HORNEY
Neurosis and Human Growth

SELF-ALIENATION refers to the inability to positively actualize and actively exercise one's personal and cultural endowments due to a lack of awareness, inhibitory fear, distortion or under-development, of those endowments. Self-alienation involves being separated from one's real self — that potentially organized and dynamically integrated set of emotional, intellectual, behavioral, social, spiritual and acquired sociohistorical capacities which, under conducive environmental/social conditions, can be used by the individual to achieve optimal well-being.

Karen Horney in her book, *Neurosis and Human Growth,* contrasts what she refers to as the *real self*, "...the original force toward individual growth and fulfillment with which we may again achieve full identification when freed of the crippling shackles of neuroses...," with the *actual self*, i.e., "...everything that a person is at a given time: body and soul, healthy and neurotic..." and the *idealized self*, i.e., "...what we are in our irrational imagination, or what we should be according to the dictates of neurotic pride."

Self-alienation is a precursory condition which allows the alienated person to be effectively manipulated to his own disadvantage and to the advantage of inimical, exploitative agents. For Blacks, these agents are their White oppressors. Self-alienation is the condition which motivates the person to internalize alien values, perspectives and other characteristics antithetical to his own interests. Through self-alienation, the alienated person acquires certain predominant ways of relating to himself, others and the world that empower those agents responsible for his self-alienation in the first place.

Self-alienation devolves from having the real self degraded, impaired, associated with negative characteristics, threats of injury or annihilation should the alienated person identify with it; having its history and future possibilities distorted, diminished; or is obscured by misidentification, falsification and denial. Furthermore, it devolves from having the alienated person's physical attributes and potentials vulgarized, associated with repulsiveness as well as other negative intellectual, emotional, behavioral, and characterological stereotypes or factors. He is frightened of self-discovery and therefore cannot attain self-fulfillment despite the fact that the means to do so may be readily available to him.

The Self-Alienated Person

The self-alienated person is not permitted to be himself. The self-alienated person cannot be for himself, cannot live for himself. He must be for and live for someone or something other than himself. He lives outside himself, besides himself. He cannot define himself. He is defined by others. He is externalized: controlled from the outside. He is not centered. His self-definition, self-concept, self-satisfaction, self-direction and happiness must be secured from outside sources. He dares not expose himself or others to his true feelings. His experiences must be artificially inseminated. Having lost contact with his true feelings he depends on other persons, alienating social rituals, consumption patterns, and the like to confirm, actualize and vitalize his alienated existence. He does not really know what he wants. His personality is as a result, filled with gaps, voids, interruptions, insatiable cravings and irrational demands.

Addicted to those persons, rituals, and things which he uses to assuage the painful insults to his alienated vanity, which he uses to temporarily allay his guilt-driven, insatiable cravings for sedation or stimulation, the self-alienated person loses wholesome self-control, self-definition, self-knowledge, self-confidence, self-acceptance, self-esteem and self-love. Consequently, he loses his freedom: his ability to exercise choice; his mastery of his destiny; his capacity to love. His is a world full of suspicion, fear, anxiety, loneliness, hypocrisy, pain and fear of pain, both conscious and unconscious. He is filled with accusations, blaming, incrimination and victimization — of himself and of others.

Because he cannot be himself, the alienated person cannot let others be themselves. He must impose his alienation on others and therefore multiply his pain and misery.

Separated from his real self, the alienated individual seeks to achieve integration and definition by claiming an artificial identity — one foisted on him by others or created from his alienated wishful thoughts and perceptions. To maintain his fictitious self-perception he must tenaciously pursue, compulsively and jealously protect and defend his imposed or wishfully-created self. The alienated person, in protecting or defending his artificial or imposed alienated self, protects and defends simultaneously, those who imposed his alienated existence on him in order to serve their material and nonmaterial interests.

The alienated person feels what he is told he should feel; desires what he is told he should desire; seeks to be the man that he is told he should be. He stands to profit from catering to his artificial feelings, desires and counterfeit manhood.

To be alienated is to hate what one has been led to perceive as one's real self, to perceive it as an enemy, to actively seek to obliterate it. Horney describes the alienated person thus:

He has an unconscious interest in not having a clear perception of himself — in making himself, as it were, deaf, dumb and blind. Not only does he blur the truth about himself but he has a vested interest in doing so — a process which blunts his sensitiveness to what is true and what is false not only inside but also outside himself.[19]

Idealization and Black-on-Black Violence

Horney's concept of the idealized self (or what we refer to herein as the fantasized self) and Freud's related concept of the ego-ideal must be further elaborated and amended if they are to be made more applicable to the psychology of oppression, particularly when the oppressor and the oppressed are of different races. Upon close examination, the concepts of self-idealization or ego-ideal are complex ones. The concepts may involve the establishment and maintenance of a fantasy or fiction in which one falsely perceives himself as relatively perfect, superior, or fully actualized.

Generally, *the idealized self* or *fantasized self* refers to what the individual perceives or fancies himself to be, or what he would like to be, how he would like to be perceived by others, to be related to by others, and how he relates to or would like to relate to others, in order to experience self-satisfaction, positive self-regard, peer acceptance, favorable personal and social distinction, as well as maximized feelings of pleasure, joy, power, security, and perhaps, feelings of superiority.

The idealized or fantasized self, or the ego-ideal, is not merely comprised of the individual's self-generated fantasies, wishes, ideas of personal perfection, or how he fancies himself to be. It includes internalized societal or cultural fantasies and ideals as well.

It is these personally and culturally acquired ideal standards against which the individual measures and evaluates himself. If the discrepancy between the way he perceives himself to be and his internalized ideals — standards against which he measures himself — are not too large, then he may experience a reasonable sense of accomplishment, self-satisfaction, and positive self-regard. If the discrepancy is too large, then he may experience feelings of failure, frustration, and self-contempt. These feelings in conjunction with other negative feelings and

---

[19] Horney, Karen. *Neurosis and Human Growth. The Struggle Toward Self-Realization.* New York: Norton, 1950.

self-perceptions, inadequate material and social resources, may produce various psychological reactions including apathy, resignation, withdrawal, anger, hostility, vindictiveness, denial and a need to fabricate and consume substitute fulfillments at any cost. The ego-ideal or fantasized self operatively exists both on the conscious and unconscious levels of the personality as do the feelings, attitudes, and behavioral orientations it generates.

Specifically, the idealized self of oppressed Africans includes internalized, projected self-idealizations of their White oppressors. By virtue of the material threats they pose against African well-being and existence, their manipulative control over the interpretation of reality, information, and other factors (the prerequisites of oppressive control), Europeans have managed to project themselves as representing the quintessence of what it means to be fully human, highly intelligent, extremely creative, supremely powerful, ultimately prestigious, and blessed by God.

Through their self-inflated projections, dominant Whites seek to arrogate to themselves — exclusively — all that is perfect and good, and to associate these perfect and good things with White skin and straight hair. The pernicious results of such associations are such that the scummiest, most reprobate of White men — by virtue of their whiteness of skin — may perceive themselves as superior to the most accomplished of Black men. Hence Black men, if they internalize projected White self-idealizations, despite all they may achieve, may still suffer a lurking sense of inferiority, or a sense of incompleteness.

The projected fraudulent, phantasmagorical idealizations of himself by the White man, and their complementary internalizations by the Black man, are necessary to the White man's successful oppression of Africans. Through these projections and their related introjection by Africans, Europeans seek to install a chronic sense of inferiority, dependency, and awe in Africans relative to themselves.

Ideally, introjection by Africans of European self-inflations and self-idealizations is designed to trick Africans into believing themselves innately inferior and to move them to accept as natural their subordination to European domination; to make them "voluntarily" keep in their designated places; to make them shrink from direct competition against Europeans, not to even dream of triumph over them; to not even think that a successful, accomplished life is possible without European approval and facilitation.

Under the influence of internalized European self-idealizations, many Blacks seek to approach projected and falsified European standards of beauty, success, and the like to the point of rejecting their own reality, their real selves and inherited ethnic characteristics; to the point of trying to relate to other Blacks in ways they perceive Whites as relating to them.

If the internalized, unconscious self-idealization or ego-ideal against which he measures himself is the Aryan White man, the Black man will always experience a sense of failure. His vain attempts to actualize his internalized, Eurocentric, reactionary idealizations promote self-alienation and his alienation from other African people. Under the alienating demands of European oppression, the oppressed reactionary African who feels entitled to a full and unimpeded measure of joy, pleasure, peer acceptance, etc., can only achieve them through manipulative, and perhaps, abrasive, violent exploitation of other African people.

Often, under the influence of his introjected idealizations, often under the alienating influence of his introjected White idealizations and of his compensatory wishful thoughts and perceptions, the oppressed African demands that others, especially other Africans, affirm his self-fantasy. If he achieves what he demands, he derives immense feelings of satisfaction. However, he is also vulnerable to feeling humiliated, insulted, robbed of pleasure and rewards, or otherwise painfully negated, when others do not play along with his demanding scenario with the requisite skill and enthusiasm.

To maintain his sense of superiority or power, his grand denial of reality, he demands perfect supporting responses from others. For perfect complementary responses by others saves him from a painful, humiliating recognition and confrontation with his diminished actual self, from having to deal with the painful reality of his situation. The perfect supporting responses of the others confirm his belief that there is nothing wrong with him, and spare him the painful necessity of self-analysis and self-reevaluation. Therefore, if supporting responses by others are not immediately forthcoming, he, feeling betrayed and offended, may physically attack them, and in the process unintentionally or intentionally kill them.

More often than not, the alienated Black man catastrophically fails to actualize his internalized, inflated European idealizations, and obtain confirmation of his reactionarily fantasied self. The resulting frustration may be so intense that in addition to destructively exploiting others to achieve a modicum of pleasure, security, and positive self-regard, he may destructively abuse his own talents and body. Failing in these respects he may opt to commit suicide.

Externalized Violence as a Mechanism of Conflict Resolution

The alienated personality is a personality in opposition to itself. It is host to a triangulated conflict between its actual, real and idealized (or fantasized) selves. Consequently, the alienated personality is disturbed. The conscious and unconscious conflict which characterizes the alienated personality is by definition, not perceived by him as occurring within himself, but is experienced by him as a disturbing process occurring between himself and the world.

Depending on a number of factors such as the degree of alienation, the type or coherence of the alienated identity he assumes, his temperament, prior socialization, type of social environment and the social class within which he operates, the alienated individual may ostensibly resolve his inner conflicts by instigating reactive, violent conflicts in his outer world.

Externalized violence may be perceived as a mechanism for conflict resolution utilized by the Black individual when he feels powerless to achieve a particular end (or set of ends) by any other means. Lacking inhibitory restraints on his violent impulses by internalized systems of moral standards, standards of conformity, lacking access to institutional or alternate means of conflict resolution, and having (more often than not) been socialized within violence-prone, overly stressful environments — the alienated Black-on-Black violent criminal may feel that he is powerless to influence or deal with his situation by any means other than violence.

Powerlessness, victimization, and proneness to violence are, under a number of circumscribed circumstances, intimately related. It is no accident that in the United States of America those alienated and stigmatized by their ethnicity, class and education/socialization, those for whom other legitimate modes of attaining social conformation of positive self-regard and self-enhancement are virtually nonexistent, whose politicoeconomic power and influence are of little or no account, are relatively more prone or likely to utilize interpersonal violence to achieve what they value than are the unstigmatized and relatively more powerful individuals or groups. By maintaining a relatively large percentage of Black Americans in the lower social strata, the White American ruling class sociopolitically instigates and structurates Black-on-Black interpersonal violence and contains it within the African American community. It then accuses that community of being inherently violent and criminal.

We should note at this juncture that the upper ruling classes are quick to utilize violence in service to the maintenance and enhancement to their positive self-regard, privileges and prerogatives. The reduced use by these classes of interpersonal, one-on-one violence, is in significant part due to the fact that they legitimatize and delegate the use of violence to their police and armed forces and other coercive institutions. These classes quite readily resort to interclass, international violence or *war* when their institutional or diplomatic systems fail to resolve certain conflicts, or when their internal conflicts, in the name of class preservation or class consciousness, cannot be otherwise resolved. The death toll, victimization, and deprivation of innocent people due to externalized upper class violence is a hundred-, thousand-, nay a million-fold, compared to that perpetrated by the lower and criminal classes in their own societies.

Self-alienation is the product of fear, anxiety, insecurity, anger, hostility, and ignorance. For these are the feelings, emotions, and states of consciousness which result from being terrorized of one's real self and of certain aspects of reality; circumstances brought on by frightening forces and people over which it does not have control.

The insecurities, fears, etc. of the self-alienated personality are chronic; they just won't go away. They go away only to come again. This is the case because these negative, nagging feelings form the infrastructure of who he is. He fears that he cannot let them go without collapsing and falling into a disorganized heap. Self-alienation involves the constant struggle against decompensation, against going to pieces, against going insane.

Because of his negatively motivated need to avoid, escape, deny, and distort his self-perception and perception of certain aspects of reality which have been either hidden from him, or associated with terror and pain by those who alienated him, the self-alienated personality, in certain crucial areas of his life and ecological existence, appears to exhibit an almost innate and incorrigible stupidity — an inability to learn from experience, an inability to guide himself according to reason. Misperceiving his real self, misperceiving large and important portions of reality, he misperceives his true interests and stupidly acts against them. He exhibits *learned* disabilities to effectively apply commonsense and intelligence in areas of his life and world which would help to achieve the goals for which he strives.

Since his alienated identity may provide him with an island of relative safety, security, and perhaps some hotly pursued recognitions, rewards, satisfactions and other factors, the self-alienated personality is prepared to struggle mightily, perhaps even kill to maintain or enhance his unauthentic self- and social-image. His alienated existence and identity were hard-won, and for that reason fiercely defended. If they were in good part achieved through ignorance, lack of awareness, the denial or severely restricted or underutilized application of intelligence and talent, then the self-alienated personality feels compelled to maintain ignorance, unconsciousness, narrow-mindedness, dumbness, servility, or ineptness — for they are his salvation. He has found that it is *smart to be dumb* about vital aspects of his life and reality. He takes pride in his foolishness. Those who attempt to help to regain his reality, to awaken to him to his state of mind, to clarify his vision, are perceived by him as deadly enemies. He therefore is prone to attack and destroy the very people who could be the source of his self-reclamation and authentic self-fulfillment.

Many self-alienated personalities "make peace" with their alienated existence and achieve a measurable sense of self-satisfaction, security, superficial happiness, and maybe love. This is particularly the case if the character of their existence and achievements fits in reasonably well with the accepted social definitions of how these things are supposed to be measured, and providing they have learned how they are supposed to behave and to feel once having made the grade. The standardized happiness, security, and the love of the self-alienated, may attain the dimensions of real feelings through their "good works" or good luck, through their consumption of material products, and failing this, through their internalization of acceptable excuses, rationalizations, and vain hopes.

But more important than these means of attaining heavenly bliss whilst in the lowest pits of alienated hell are the good feelings the self-alienated attain through successfully distancing themselves from ugly reality, through successfully repressing out of their consciousness disturbing contradictions. The more distanced, the more repressed, the better the feelings.

However, there are many alienated personalities whose distance or separation from their real self and reality is not complete, or not consistently successful enough to afford them the alienated peace, happiness, security, and love they so desperately seek. Their confused and painful confrontations with their actual conditions are exceedingly stressful. Unwanted, disturbing reality keeps breaking through their defense perimeters. Their state is one of crisis. Their existence is tenuous, tense, and conflicted. Their unsteady balance is often made to swing wildly by any rather slight changes in their inner or outer world. The ground constantly shifts under their feet.

This, in part, describes the state of the Black-on-Black violent criminal.

This self-alienated individual in crisis has, as far as he can see, all his legitimate escape routes away from the self he has learned to fear, blocked by barriers he cannot legitimately or quickly overcome. These impregnable obstacles seem to repel him backwards toward the horrifying reality from which he is trying to escape. The barriers themselves remind him of the reality he wishes so hopelessly to avoid. They are the nature of his body, the color of his skin, texture of his hair. They are his nativity. They are the symbolic sources of his fears and the barriers to his escape. He is caged. He is furious. And his fury grows exponentially as he struggles to break free from the trap that seems to grip him all the more painfully tight the more he struggles to be free.

But he refuses to give in. He refuses to be the hunter's game. His self-alienated pride and vanity have been affronted and he seeks revenge. He resents those who seem to have resigned to their captivity, and who have yielded themselves to be sacrificed. He wants to turn the tables — to become the hunter, not the hunted. He may not know who he is but knows he is not supposed to be where he is. He knows someone dealt him a bad hand before he knew the rules of the game; that he is supposed to be the "fall guy," the patsy. These he refuses to be, at risk of incarceration or at risk of his life. He will be nobody's fool. He knows that in being instrumentalized and objectified by the world for its fun and profit, the world owes him something. He is determined to collect C.O.D.

7

INCULCATING THE BEAST

"The father you spring from is the
devil
and willingly you carry out his
wishes.
He brought death to man from the
beginning,
and has never based himself on truth;
the truth is not in him.
Lying speech is his native tongue
he is a liar and the father of lies."

JOHN 8:44

The Father, the Son, and the Unholy Spirit

THE PSYCHOLOGICAL COMPLEX is the father of the child and of
the man. To possess a complex is to be possessed by that complex.
According to Freud, the child becomes a man-child when the
Oedipus complex is resolved through introjection and acceptance;
when external governing complexes become internal governing
complexes. The individually psychological is but the actualized,
delimited transfiguration of the collectively sociological; the
political personalized. The biological father is not necessarily
the psycho-spiritual father. And it is the psycho-spiritual father

105

who is the father in the truest psychological sense because it is his psychogenetic inheritance that is actualized in the body, mind, soul, and behavior of the son.

The psycho-spiritual, and therefore true psychological father of the violent Black-on-Black criminal, is the racist White American man. The American Black-on-Black criminal is the psychological son of the White-on-Black criminal who does the work of the Eurocentric patriarch who sired him.

> *Black man, you who inflict pain on yourself,*
> *your mothers, your fathers, sisters, brothers,*
> *and your children*
> *Know that you are criminal because you wish*
> *to identify with your crimogenic*
> *Eurocentric father and do not know, and*
> *therefore cannot love, your African self*
> *Know that you are the child and manservant of*
> *the Father of lies!*

In order for Blacks to assault, rape, rob, and murder each other with notorious and self-destructive intensity, to be estranged from their own bodies and therefore subject them to all manner of health and physical carelessness, neglect and self-mediated abuse; to make them hosts to all manner of insatiably unhealthy appetites, they must internalize Eurocentric racist hostility toward themselves; internalize and claim as their own the European contempt for the color of their skin and the physiognomy of their bodies. These Blacks must take Eurocentric lies for truth and truth for lies and act accordingly. They must see their bodies as the cause of pain and as their enemy, and consequently subject them to disrespect and murderous mutilation. They will destroy others who are clothed in a body like their own for they must be the enemy too. The Black-on-Black violent criminal experiences this dilemma with full intensity for he has internalized the lies of his racist White fathers most deeply.

In his vain attempts to avoid, deny and escape the internalized contempt of his White racist fathers and the unbearable pain and suffering of subordination, to relieve the rage which comes from impotence, contempt for self and others like himself, he is compelled to identify with the originator of his pain, his creator, and becomes his White progenitor's ally in a full-scale assault on himself and his people. He thinks that in imitating his White racist creator he can vicariously appropriate his power and privilege, his prestige and material comforts, his alleged "humanness," and above all, escape his "niggerness." For he has learned well the lessons taught him while at the feet of his White racist father; that it is his body, his alleged "niggerness," which is the source of his agonizing subordination. He was not given to know that he suffers not because of his "blackness" but because his White racist father is a psychopath. Skin color, texture of hair, fullness of lips, broadness of nose cannot be the "cause" of inferiority and pain: only other men, things and creatures.

> *You are possessed by the Lust, Vanity,*
> *and Greed of your White racist father*
> *And like him, you greed to deny the poor*
> *and powerless the meager benefits*
> *of their lands and labors*
>
> *You snatch from their mouths*
> *and those of their children*
> *the bread they earned by the barely*
> *recompensed sweat of their brows*
> *Like your White racist father*
> *you lust to uncaringly exploit the bodies*
> *of the weak and the unprotected*
>
> *You vainly attempt to satiate*
> *your insatiable vanity by degrading*
> *your own whom you disown*
> *Like your White racist father,*
> *you raise yourself high by standing*
> *on the accumulated bodies of those*
> *you have brought low*

The Paradox of Identification

In identifying with his White racist father and thereby seeking to escape the onerous conditions of his subordination, the Black-on-Black exploitative and violent criminal does not so much seek to deny his color and assume the coloration of his White father as he wishes to identify with the true source of his White racist father's superiority-independence gained through his power to violently exercise his will on others (which includes his power to treat "niggers" any way he feels). While the possession of material comforts and luxuries, of recognition, "admiration," "respect," etc., may be associated with the whiteness of European skin, it is with his will to and capacity for violence that the Black-on-Black criminal wishes to identify in his White racist father. It is the complementary powerlessness and its associated material deprivations and discomforts, the will to and capacity for nonviolence and suffering by Black peoples that is the object of his contempt and from which he wishes to escape by assuming a will to power all his own, and independent of others. He, like his White racist father, wishes to be his own man.

While he imitates his White father he resents his father's power and his own subjugation to it, and at the same time holds utter contempt for his own cowardice, for he does not dare to take power from his father. He holds contempt for people who hide their cowardice behind the facade of morality and "law abiding" behavior. Like all bullies, like his White racist father — the world's greatest bully — he is at heart a coward. Like all cowards and bullies, he pummels the defenseless. He cowers at learning the skills necessary for overthrowing his tyrannical White racist overlords. He does not possess the blood and guts to stand up to his own weaknesses and lack of courage. He is loud, "courageous," and boastful when attacking his prey in the darkness of night and in deserted streets, and when he speaks disgracefully of his own peoples.

The Black-on-Black violent criminal knows, consciously or subconsciously, that it is his White psycho-spiritual father's monopoly on violence that is the key to his dominance. He knows that his Eurocentric racist father is but a barely disguised criminal who "cons" through manipulative lies and deceptions; whose criminal actions are self-legitimized by his power; who commits wholesale domestic oppression, global thuggery and mass murder by proxy through the manipulative use of his domestic draconian police and imperial armed forces. He knows that his racist White father, if judged by the rule that a criminal is *he who violates a criminal code*, is by far and away the most criminal of people; that he violates the hundreds of codes he himself has instituted. The Black-on-Black criminal knows that the "criminal codes" he violates are first of all, those he had no part in enacting, and secondly, are relatively minuscule and cover only a minute portion of the voluminous criminal codes written by his White fathers. He knows that he is not permitted to be in the position to violate the majority of the codes, let alone exonerate himself from prosecution and penalty if, like his White father, he violates them. More importantly, he knows that the "laws" of his Eurocentric fathers are not the laws of God or of Humanity, but are the "laws" designed to protect and continue the White monopoly on violence and exploitative domination. He knows that his White narcissistic father is a "law onto himself," that for the White man "the State is me" and as the State he has usurped the legitimate monopoly on power and the right to use it against any and all in the name of protecting his interests, and the right to behave criminally in the name of maintaining "law and order." The Black-on-Black criminal, with his internalized self-contempt and general resentment, peremptorily assumes the violent prerogatives of his White racist fathers.

Because he regards the ordinary legal codes as a charade that legitimizes unwarranted privilege, because he lives in a fundamentally immoral sociopolitical system not of his making, he rejects as a sham the values and customs of the larger White-dominated society. As a result of focused observation, modeling, and copycatting of the hypocritical and morally unacceptable values and customs of his White racist parents, and because of his internalized White racist father's contempt for his people, the Black-on-Black criminal feels free to exploitatively abuse them and others without compunction. Through his contemptuous treatment of other "law abiding" Blacks ("wimps" or "chumps" in his eyes), the Black-on-Black criminal futilely attempts to transcend his own "blackness." He seeks to become a member in an exclusive club and gains a novel sense of belonging, an in-group sense of superiority. Through his illicit acts he achieves, or attempts to achieve, the psychological satisfaction of having successfully outwitted his White racist father and distinguished himself from the downtrodden masses, as well as perhaps gaining monetary and other rewards and privileges.

Pained by both his subordination to his White racist father and his contempt for the weakness and humiliation of his people, by his self-contempt, the Black-on-Black malefactor (who may often, but significantly less frequently, engage in Black-on-White or indiscriminate violence), like his White racist father, seeks to become a law onto himself; to be the source of his own rewards. He is driven to demonstrate his superiority above all law and custom and sees his ego salvation as independent of the approval and acceptance of others. He lacks respect for all others, except those like himself who seek to monopolize violence and use it to further their interests. He perceives himself as having no obligatory loyalties to any individuals, groups or social values — especially if these entities are African American like himself. He, like his White racist master, does not permit himself to feel guilty, and like his Eurocentric racist master, may gain a perverse sense of satisfaction in acting out his impulsive, irresponsible, callous, self-centered urgings on his Black victims. He has no patience with "niggers."

His dominance is measured by his demonstrable ability to gain the "upper hand," "beat the other to the punch." He sees control and power, as well as his unhesitating ability to use violence, as the only sure way of preventing his abuse and humiliation at the hands of others. Feeling betrayed by his people, humiliated by their low-status and weakness, by their "niggerness," he "punishes" and humiliates them further. Through the power of violence he seeks retribution: to "get back" through vindictive anger and violence at those who mistreated and betrayed him, and who, if he were "weak" and "soft," would exploit him and do him harm. The sentiments of his White racist father exactly!

The most exploitative and abusive Black-on-Black criminal is one whose internalization of White racist contempt for African peoples has been so painfully and incontrovertibly absorbed until while imitating the violence-prone, exploitative orientation of his White racist models, he rejects out-of-hand the introjection and active acceptance of their self-serving and restraining "conscience" and its attendant feelings of guilt and shame. He identifies with no one except his own barely controlled cravings, excitements, and chronic search for pleasure. He and his impulses are one. His love, if it exists, is an exploitative love; a "using" love. He knows no loyalties to culture or community, to friendships or other emotional ties except those which serve his twisted needs and desires. He craves the omnipotence, supremacy, and arrogant self-assurance of his White racist father — the archetypal sociopath! Having surrendered his inner substance and self-control to his White racist father, and having rejected his fundamental ethnocultural identity, he eschews responsibility, reliability, and binding agreements. He abandons with reckless disregard friends and family in his selfish pursuit of ephemeral pleasure.

Identification and Alienation

Identification refers to a process whereby a subject consciously or unconsciously takes on what he presumes to be the distinguishing characteristics (attitudes, styles of behavior, emotions and feelings, modes of dress, status symbols) of another whom he holds in high-esteem and/or fears. By assuming the behavioral attitudes and attributes of his model, the subject comes to feel that he has also absorbed some of his model's power and prestige, can exercise his model's authority, advantages, and privileges. Behaving as if he *were* his imitative model, particularly when or if rewarded for doing so, the subject enhances his feelings of worth and dignity. In this instance, he uses the process of identification to defend his ego and self-image against self-devaluation and negative evaluation by others.

The subject undergoes the process of identification because he recognizes the fact that the perception of others and their evaluation of him are significantly influenced by their view of him as being a member of, or the degree to which he exhibits the characteristics associated with a high prestige and powerful group. Conversely, his and others evaluation of himself may be markedly influenced by the degree to which he is not viewed as a member of, or exhibits the characteristics associated with, a group which lacks power or prestige. Thus, the subject may enhance his own feelings of adequacy and worth by associating himself with a highly regarded class, group, and individual, and/or by distancing himself or denying any substantial relation to a class, group, or individual who may be negatively regarded or socially ostracized by others.

In America, where power, prestige, pulchritude, advantage and privilege are firmly associated with White Americans, and the opposite of these factors associated with African Americans, many members of the latter group, to varying degrees, seek by a number of psychological and behavioral means and other ruses to associate themselves with White Americans and/or at least to dissociate themselves from their African heritage and identity. Association with such a heritage and identity evokes in these subjects intense feelings of inferiority, insecurity, incompetence, cursedness, powerlessness and worthlessness. Enhancing self-regard, social acceptance, and positive self-feeling by identifying with an alien group or individual whose interests are inimical to oneself and group, if taken too far, is ultimately self-defeating and injurious to others. The use of identification with inappropriate models, (e.g., White Americans in order to escape or avoid reality, and in order to maintain feelings of adequacy and self-worth) over time leads victimized African Americans to develop an unrealistic and inaccurate perception of themselves and of reality: both of which will ultimately render their behavior maladaptive, antisocial and self-destructive. Finally, they may suffer the humiliation they so dread because their identification with their racist White masters is not accepted by those masters. Consequently, many African Americans may come to feel as if they have been painfully used, abused, betrayed, and/or rejected by those with whom they have attempted to identify.

Identification with the Aggressor

The particular form of identification utilized in the above discussion of the violent Black-on-Black criminal is referred to as *identification with the aggressor.* In this instance, identification is utilized by the subject to avoid negative consequences, (e.g., injury, fear, anxiety) and feelings of self-depreciation brought on by what the subject considers a powerful, actually or potentially-abusive, life-threatening, arbitrary, tyrannical aggressor. The subject seeks to master his anxieties, vulnerabilities, and sense of inferiority by identifying with the threatening individual or group, imitating what he assumes to be his model's salient attributes. These attributes may include some of the aggressor's values, physical features, attributes, status symbols, symbols of strength and aggressive behavior. Through identification with the aggressor the subject attempts to magically transform himself from the one threatened into to one who threatens; from powerless to powerful; inferior to superior. Concomitant with his identification with the aggressor, the subject's emotional distress and status anxiety is allayed, and he delusively removes himself from a position of helpless passivity to one of relative autonomous activity.

The change in self-perception attained through his identifying with the aggressor allows him to dis-identify and disclaim his prior threatened identity or membership in the threatened group. By fantasying himself the aggressor and not the victim, and by disavowing his membership in the victimized group, the subject may assume an attitude towards his group similar to that assumed by the aggressor, with whom he identifies. Having internalized the aggressor's values, attitudes, and having imitated aspects of the aggressor's negative behavior toward himself as victim, and thereby assuming the identity and prerogatives of the aggressor, the subject "feels free" to treat or mistreat other victims like himself the way they are treated by his aggressor model. The oppressed subject seeks to identify with his aggressor, his aggressor's arbitrary and unimpeded behavior, and his symbols of that behavior. He believes these factors represent the essence of freedom, what it means *to be*; to be "free"; to be independent; to be exempt from, and immune to, degradation by others.

As intimated by Paulo Freire in his book, *Pedagogy of the Oppressed*, the oppressed "...have a diffuse, magical belief in the invulnerability and power of the oppressor." He further states:

> The oppressed suffer from the duality which has established itself in their innermost being. They discover that without freedom they cannot exist authentically. Yet, although they desire authentic existence, they fear it. They are at one and the same time themselves and the oppressor whose conscious-ness they have internalized. The conflict lies in the choice between being wholly themselves or being divided; between ejecting the oppressor within or not ejecting him; between human solidarity and alienation; between following prescrip-tions or having choices; between being spectators or actors; between acting or having the illusion of acting through the action of the oppressors; between speaking out or being silent, castrated in their power to create and re-create, in their power to transform the world.[20]

---

[20] Freire, Paulo. *Pedagogy of the Oppressed*. New York: Continuum, 1983.

Freire tellingly depicts how some oppressed subjects assume that to be free, "to be somebody," means *"to be is to be like,* and *to be like* is *to be like the oppressor, ..."* This definition of freedom, of "beingness," is at center of the dangerous dilemma the Black-on-Black criminal represents in the African American community — and society in general. Through identification with the aggressor White racist, who he erroneously believes to be the apotheosis of what it means to be free and superior, he chooses *to be like* his, and his people's, most deadly enemy. The logic escapes him that if freedom and superiority mean to behave like one's deadliest enemy, if the aggressor's freedom and superiority is based on the brutal subordination and victimization of him and his people, then his imitative freedom must likewise rest on his brutal oppression and exploitation of his own people, and more paradoxically, on his oppression, exploitation and victimization of himself.

Having identified with the aggressor White racist, the violent Black-on-Black criminal foolishly allies himself with the enemy of his people and of himself, and helps to maintain their, as well as his own, subordination. The fear of humiliation and possibly of annihilation, the fear of nothingness, the avoidance of feelings of anxiety and vulnerability he seeks to allay through participating in the charade of identifying with his White tormentors, and/or "dis-identifying" with his people and Africanness, are only temporarily alleviated. His imminent incarceration and death sentence are only momentarily stayed. For the deluded freedom of an alienated existence, the illusory freedom and majesty attained through identification with one's enemies represents in reality the purest form of slavery or half freedom — freedom only to do the wrong thing, to do harm to oneself, one's people, and the world.

This kind of freedom is the freedom of a criminal — no freedom at all.

Through committing homicide the Black-on-Black criminal, steeped in his existential, internalized White supremacist-instigated guilt, often seeks his own death. He desperately searches for his executioner. He provokes others to do what he himself dares not to do — to kill him as a way of killing himself, as a way of committing suicide. He is determined that his subliminal guilt must not go unpunished. So he places himself in harm's way. He compels himself to live dangerously. He falls for the ultimate sting. Carrying another man's guilt, he pretends to live without it. He thinks himself a black pantherized predator, when in reality he has been chumped into playing the part of a sacrificial lamb. All for nothing!

> *You sire uncared-for sons and daughters*
> *Because, like your hedonistic White racist father*
> *You perceive the bodies of your peoples to be*
> *the fleshpots of your pleasures*
> *Bones to be sucked of their marrow and*
> *chucked away caring nothing of consequences*
> *You dare not victimize your victimizer*
> *You deign only to victimize yourself*
> *And make victims of the victimized*

Displaced Aggression

We have discussed the fact that through denying, distorting, and rationalizing their own criminality in their own community, White Americans utilize every means at their disposal — their socioeconomic, psychopolitical, military and propagandistic supremacy — to project a matrix of highly organized negative stereotypical images, characterizations, and other falsified perceptions onto the bodies and into the psyches of African American peoples. Negative stereotyping conjoined with the imposition of negative residential, occupational, social, educational, experiential circumstances on Black America, are combined in order to implant a reactionary "spirit" in the collective African American body and psyche. One of the major functions of this alien implant is to render ineffective, or deflect, retaliatory responses by the Black community away from its White racist creators. The alienation of the African American psyche is most effectively achieved by blinding the African American to the machinations of the original instigators of his condition and by directing his reactionary hostility toward those not responsible for his predicament. Because of the introjected spirit with which the Black-on-Black criminal identifies, he, like his White creators, will blame his Black victims.

In the minds of victimized African Americans and the Black-on-Black criminal, the introjected White racist spirit exaggerates the power of its White creators, making them appear near invincible, as vital to the continuity of "law and order," to the maintenance of "life, liberty and the pursuit of happiness," and to self-acceptance. Simultaneously, it induces them to exaggerate their ostensible powerlessness and incapacity to develop a world superior to that of their White exploiters. Moreover, the White racist spirit which possesses them evokes self-doubt and fear of annihilation whenever they dare consider the overthrow of their European oppressor, or dare to raise their collective hands against those Europeans who spitefully use them. Yet this spiteful use occurs as it must under oppression and exploitation. Being spitefully used provokes in African Americans retributive and retaliatory anger, and the need to disarm and neutralize their oppressors. Since this anger often cannot be fully expressed against its White instigators for fear of annihilation, and yet must be expressed and relieved, it must of necessity be redirected toward other objects. The objects of the Black-on-Black violent criminal's hostility — because of their proximity and their inability to effectively defend themselves, because they are more likely to be inadequately defended by others, and their abuse unlikely to be severely punished — will most likely to be other Blacks. It is by means of this type of displaced and gratuitous violence that the White instigators of that violence shield themselves against effective retaliation by the beleaguered African American community. Furthermore, the oppressive White American community gains the added benefit of having its racist stereotypes actualized in the African American psyche, thereby lending substance to their rationalizations for the oppression of African Americans and Africans in general. Moreover, these actualization and rationalization processes permit their White racist instigators to "legitimately" rid themselves of the most aggressive Black males — the ones more likely under other circumstances to challenge their dominance — by incarcerating them and by motivating them to engage in mutual annihilation. These Black-on-Black violent miscreants, by generating and maintaining a relatively high level of mistrust, hostility and criminality in the African community, unwittingly assist its White racist oppressors in maintaining the requisite level of social disorganization in that community and as such make its collective unification and development for their overthrow highly unlikely. Ultimately, if intensified, such misdirected, wrongly recompensed, inward-directed hostility represented as Black-on-Black violence, could bring the Black community to the point of "self-destruction" or "self-annihilation," — thereby assuaging White American guilt and absolving in its collective mind its responsibility for instigating and sustaining its genocidal activities against the African American community.

To Be An African Male In America

To be an African male in America is to be a frustrated man. To be an African male is to be an angry male; an enraged man, whether or not the anger and rage are consciously acknowledged. For many African American men, these feelings lie deeply submerged beneath layers of repression and hidden behind an unperturbable or friendly facade, only finding outlet and expression in a hundred ordinary annoyances and petty gripes. For many other African American men, these feelings lie preconsciously beneath a deceptively inscrutable public persona, strenuously held there by social and religious inhibitions and fears of injurious or deadly consequences should those feelings be "inappropriately" revealed or repressed. The subdued anger and rage are kept in place by a cautious and wary avoidance of provocative circumstances and through the diligent application of selective inattention to be a world filled with provocative potential. For these men, anger and rage are sublimated, redirected, compensated, and diverted into "productive" activities. But there are also those men whose anger and rage are apparent, threatening to erupt volcanically into the atmosphere. You see it in their truculence. You hear it in their strident and impatient voices. You witness it in their daunting stares and in the tautness of their movements. Some run about like carriers of time-bombs looking for a place to explode. Others are pressure cookers needing to release a head of steam.

To be an African American male is to be confronted with bedeviling contradictions. It is to live with chronic feelings of self-consciousness; to experience the emptiness of deprivation; to be more often than not unfulfilled, unactualized and depotentiated. To be an African American male is to be ethnoculturally insulted; to be mentally and morally underestimated; to be the object of the irrational and unpredictable hostility of others; to be perceived as a breathing, red-blooded stereotype; to be looked through; to be often regressed because the avenues of healthy self-expression and personal potentiation are closed against positive forward movement.

To be an African American male is to be singled out for intense and sadistic frustration; to be psychologically castrated, emasculated and feminized; to have your group and personal coin always devalued; to see your people praying hard, singing loud and long, ecstatically moaning, groaning, shouting, fainting, and groveling before a hand-me-down *god* who seems to reward their spirited devotion with ever-increasing deprecations, while those who flout the authority of that god are overloaded with earthly powers and possessions. Under such circumstances it is not difficult to feel that the very heavens themselves are conspiring against African manhood.

Frustration and Aggression

Frustration refers to being prevented from achieving a desired objective by obstructing natural or social barriers, or by personal limitations. Many personal limitations may be the result of negative interpersonal, intergroup, and/or other more or less deliberately designed psychopolitical interactions and hindrances. Among other predispositions, frustration often generates an aggressive response towards the perceived source of frustration. It is energized by anger and hostile attitudes. Frustration and its attendant anger define the existential condition of the African American under White American socioeconomic oppression.

Many frustrated African American males may deny their anger or translate it into various forms of dependency and passivity, desperate withdrawal and resignation, psychosomatic and self-mediated illnesses, religious narcosis, and self-anesthetization. Others seek to alleviate their anger through the ingestion of inebriants and psychoactive palliatives, sexual and musical addictions, overcompensatory achievements and attempts at constructive problem-solving. Yet there are other males who strike out in furious anger, giving primal expression to their rage. Tragically, it is this misdirected, misunderstood, unsublimated rage and aggression which, instead of motivating the throttling of the source of their frustrations and the neutralizing of their oppressors, unwittingly strengthens them.

Displaced, misdirected Black rage and violence has many progenitors. Among them: (1) cowardice before what is perceived as an indomitable oppressor; (2) dependency on those who revile them; (3) the difficulty of actualizing the power capable of defeating their enemies; (4) the intangibility, vagueness and covertness of White American perfidy; (5) feelings of inadequacy, incompetence, cursedness; (6) the need to gain a sense of self-esteem and masculinity at any price; (7) the absence of opportunities and social institutions for self-expression and actualization of hope; (8) perception of other Blacks as "chumps" and "wimps" who deserve mistreatment; (9) a sense of having been betrayed by ancestors and elders, who through their own failings and wrongheadedness, passivity and perverted love for those who persecuted them, have bequeathed to their progeny, empty hopes, empty pockets, poverty and powerlessness. These feelings and perceptions together create in the angry Black-on-Black criminal a lack of respect for his own ethnocultural background and milieu, an absence of respect for others in general, and an absence of respect for himself. He feels he owes no one anything. He often thinks of himself as virtually worthless. Often at the extremity of his thinking he feels that if he loses his life he loses nothing and if he takes the lives of others, especially others like himself, he has taken nothing.

For the angry Black man overwhelmed by displaced aggressive passions, other Blacks fulfill their chosen roles — that of scapegoats, sacrificial lambs, bearers of the cross for other peoples' sins, recipients and carriers of others' and his own displaced hostilities and aggressions. Threatened by backlash should he attack Whites for their obvious misdeeds, the enraged Black-on-Black criminal often turns away from his original White supremacist instigators to assuage his anger on his fellow Black victims. His manhood in question, his sensitivity to the slightest humiliation heightened, his need to cathartically rid himself of his anger, he determines that even though "the Man" may pick on him and get away with it, he "ain't gon' let a nigger git away wit messin' over me." The Black-on-Black criminal, as he destroys his substitute Black victims, destroys himself. He assaults them because he is ultimately possessed and under the influence of his White racist introjected devil who directs his attack away from his White persecutors and onto his fellow victims.

Frustration can and does produce a number of consequences of which hostile aggression is only one. Generally, the hostile aggressive reactions to frustration may be of two types — direct and displaced. *Direct hostile aggression* refers to the situation wherein reactionary aggression is focused directly against the perceived cause and source of frustration. Should the cause or source remain hidden, ambiguous, intangible, or more commonly, so powerful that a hostile aggressive attack against it would expose the attacker to severely painful retaliatory injuries, deprivations, injurious losses of various types, and possible annihilation, that attack may be re-directed toward some object, person, or group other than the original cause or source of frustration. This type of re-directed hostile aggression is referred to as *displaced hostile aggression*. In this instance, the aggressive individual or party, pressed by anger and a compelling need to express that anger, yet constrained from expressing it directly, finds partial release by attacking a less dangerous target.

Displaced aggression not only allows the frustrated individual to cathartically re-direct his hostility toward some innocent person or group, but also helps him to sustain or regain a sense of self-esteem while palliating his sense of helplessness, passivity, victimization, loss of control and status. Through his treatment of others as he himself is treated, the frustrated aggressor may perceive himself as an equal to his frustrator, and hence identify with his *frustrator / aggressor.*

Through fear of challenging directly the source of his frustration, his identification with and internalization of some of his frustrator's values and attitudes, the frustrated aggressive individual may find a scapegoat who can be blamed for his problems and who is perceived as not capable of effective retaliation. This is someone who has no powerful protector, whose rights of retaliation are constrained, and the penalty for whose injury will remain relatively lightly punished or go unpunished. In these instances, displaced aggression provides a means of expressing dangerously hostile feelings while incurring relatively little or no risk of retaliation. Displaced aggression also enables the frustrated aggressive individual to hold his more powerful frustrator in relative high (or envious) regard and as worthy of imitation. It further enables him to view his frustrator as relatively blameless, while blaming the victim of his displaced hostility for his discontents.

The violent Black-on-Black criminal provides a premier example of a severely frustrated individual who hostilely expresses misdirected aggression. This victim of White American narcissistic racism finds his scapegoats in his fellow victims. Like the White supremacists whose values, attitudes, etc., he has internalized and incarnates, he dehumanizes his African American victims as a prelude to, and rationalization for, their exploitation. Identified with the White supremacist establishment which spawned him through its abusive, insulting, degrading, exploitative, overbearing, and castrating intercourse with his people, he turns on his own people. Having internalized the egregiously evil and hostile attitudes of the White supremacist establishment, he seeks vainly to prove his "manhood" by brutally attacking and exploiting other Black men and women. Terrorized by White supremacy, he creates his own terror — the petty terrors of small-time criminals, tyrants, muggers, household dictators, and emasculated bullies trying to act like the "big boys."

His mind and perceptions dulled by his Eurocentric miseducation, or the lack of an Afrocentric one, the violent Black-on-Black criminal cannot see through the mental and political pettifoggery which obscures the many ways the White supremacist establishment so torturously frustrates him. He can feel the effects of his frustration but not fathom their sources. Frustration which motivates hostile aggression is all the more compelling for the fact that its sources are hidden and can only be projected or externalized onto the most convenient targets: targets he can see — his neighbors, his lovers, his people. Thus, he allies with his White frustrators in an unrelenting attack on himself and his people. His criminality provides his oppressors with rationales for their incarceration or annihilation of him, and their continuing political/economic, intellectual/cultural subordination and mercenary genocide of African American people. And thus, White America "kills two birds with one stone": the violent Black-on-Black criminal which it created and the African American community which it dominates.

Your freedom is the superbal expression of slavery
   — the freedom of slaves
You are free to speak as long as no one listens
   Free to explain as long as no one understands

Free to sing and dance as long as you entertain
        those who would have you sing and dance
            on a tightrope above an open grave
Free to think as long as you think feelings
        Free to love as long as it is your tormentors
            and not yourself that you love
Free to assemble as long as you gather together
        to screw each other
Free to engage in self-defense as long as it is truth
        and reality against which you defend yourself
Free to kiss as long as you kiss the ass of
        the one who offends you
You have the right to a fair trial before a jury of
        your peers as long as you are a criminal
You are free to spend your money as you like
        as long as you like to spend it
            with those who spitefully use you
Who use it to finance your execution
        and to bury you in your store-bought finest

8

CHASING THE AMERICAN MIRAGE

He was spurned and avoided by men,
a man of suffering, accustomed to infirmity,
One of those from whom men hide their faces,
spurned, and we held him in no esteem.
Yet it was our infirmities that he bore,
our sufferings that he endured,
While we thought of him as stricken,
as one smitten by God and afflicted,
But he was pierced for our offenses,
crushed for our sins;
Upon him was the chastisement
that makes us whole,
by his stripes we were healed.

ISAIAH 53:3-5

The Production of Desire

MANY PERSONS FIND IT COMFORTING to think of the criminal as "different," as being distinctly not the same as the "law-abiding" citizen. It is common to perceive the criminal as possessing a "criminal personality," a pathological personality which is discontinuous with the personality of the "average," "normal" individual. The criminal is more often than not, perceived as one compelled by "criminal" desires, drives, needs, and nefarious motivations which flow from intrinsic psychological imbalances. The search for, and delineation of, the "criminal personality," — of the definitive "criminal profile" — has been a long and tireless one in European history. Such an endeavor presupposes that there exists a constellation of personality characteristics or dispositions which, regardless of sociocultural or experiential context, motivates a person who possesses that confluence of characteristics or traits, to commit crimes. This type of presupposition relative to other matters such as the diagnosing and classification of witches, the phrenological determination of character, the proving of the intellectual inferiority of Blacks, etc., has its own history, particularly in Western Europe. That tradition continues alive and well in White American academia and folk psychology. A study of the vicissitudes of such presuppositions relative to their political and power relations contexts, can be exceedingly instructive.

One obvious conclusion drawn from such a study is the fact that such presuppositions, such as a "criminal personality," often are invented by persons, organizations and societies as ways of denying their responsibility for creating the "personality" which they so self-righteously condemn. This type of presupposition allows them the luxury of not recognizing the inextricable relatedness to themselves to those others they condemn or find reprehensible. Furthermore, this allows the condemned personalities to be treated reprehensibly, or in extreme circumstances, to be liquidated in good conscience with the sense of social cleansing, purgation, and eugenic purification of the body politic by "well-meaning" citizens and professionals. Consequently, the rectification of criminality endemic to American society may conceivably be accomplished without the rectification of the American social order. The social order, of which criminality is a social symptom, is not called into question.

In light of the foregoing, it is easy to understand why the White American community is so readily seduced by the ideology that the Black-on-Black criminal is "compelled" by an inherited personality syndrome, a set of intrinsically instigated and organized criminal drives, needs, values, attitudes, tendencies, orientations, etc., which have little or nothing to do with his sociohistorical experience of being Black in White America.

However, a cursory examination of human motivation soon convinces us that human behavior is by far more instigated, oriented, and regulated by anticipations, temptations, enticements, and incentives, than by internal drives, needs or deprivations. Human behavior is more "pulled" than "pushed," i.e., impelled by external forces and their internal representations than the other way around. One does not desire or seek to consume strawberry ice-cream before one has ever heard of it. One rarely eats it because one "needs" to do so. However, once having conceived it, having seen it, or having tasted it, one may afterward become subjected to a "desire," "a need," "a compelling drive," to obtain and consume it. Knowing it conceivably or actually exists may now "create" in the desiring person a sense of deprivation, of lack, of need or "taste" it.

The violent ghetto criminal did not have a desire for and willingness to kill to obtain a pair of expensive sneakers before they conceivably or actually existed. The sneakers (product) must have been imaginatively or actually presented to him in such a way that his desire and willingness to kill for them were elicited and activated by their presentation. Thus, in some way his desire and related behavior is intrinsically tied to the production and presentation of things external to himself; not a pre-existing criminal desire or disposition without cause, or precipitating object or objective. We thirst for and need water, not because we were thirsty first and because water was created to satisfy our thirst, but because we are water creatures: created in and evolved from a water environment. Water existed prior to thirst for it. Analogously, society is prior to the individual; the individual is submerged in society and is to a significant extent a created product of it. His desires and needs are consequently social and societal productions and can only be satisfied within some set of social parameters. Individual desires are at heart social desires.

Man is uniquely idolatrous. He invests Nature and his creations with symbolic power and proceeds to become subject to the power he imputes to them. The desires and feelings evoked in himself by such transactions with symbolized Nature and created objects may then be perceived by him as operating autonomously, independently of those entities, as existing prior to their symbolization (or man-made creation). This trait of Man allows those who create and produce objects, images and conditions which elicit desires and behaviors in others — those who have a vested interest in the status quo — to attribute those evoked desires and related behavior, (if inimical to their interests), to the "evil character" or motives of the condemned individual or group, to the Devil, or to some principle operating in the world independent of Mankind: never to the social order which they themselves created and seek to preserve at all costs. In other words, desires which have been deliberately created or manufactured, are often afterward perceived as independently pre-existing by their creators or manufacturers. This is most likely to occur when the latter wish to profit from their creations while not taking responsibility for the danger their existence may represent.

The Black-on-Black criminal desires those things the White American ruling class tells him are desirable. He values those things White American society designates as valuable. His personal needs are social needs. He is the creation of the White American social status quo; not of any inherent criminal character of African American people. His desires, needs, deprivations, and other supposed factors which compel his criminality are manufactured, scripted, organized and regulated through White American material and social production. African American needs, tastes, lacks, deprivations, empty spaces, are instigated and sustained by a pre-existing, White American organized, owned and controlled, production and politicoeconomic system. Hence, Black-on-Black "criminal" needs are essentially the *same* as those exhibited by all "noncriminal" Americans. Generally they are artificial, i.e., "the deliberate creation of lack as a function of market economy [which] is the art of a [White American] dominant class." This involves deliberately organizing wants and needs "...amid an abundance of production; making all desire teeter and fall victim to the greater fear of not having one's needs satisfied ..."[21]

The fantasies, desires and needs which supposedly motivate Black-on-Black criminal behavior and the behavior of other members of the American system, are dependent on the production and presentation of real things, and are therefore not merely

[21] Deleuze, S., & Guatarri, *Anti-Oedipus: Capitalism and Schizophrenia*. Minneapolis: MIT Press, 1983.

mental, "free-floating" states of consciousness cut-off from the operations of the White-owned and controlled market economy.

The structuration of social production is *equivalent* to the construction and structuration of desire. Social production is desiring production. The structuration of desire, the organized production and presentation of objects, conditions, and situations which evoke desire, is tantamount to organizing desire in ways which support the system of production and its related social order. African American desires, tastes, and needs are so evoked and organized by White American manufactured products, marketing strategies and social status concepts that their attempted and accomplished satisfaction maintains the very system which oppresses them. Through the White American structuration of their desires by means of material and social production, African Americans come to *desire*, to *want*, to *need* White American dominance and control of the productive forces on which their very physical and social lives depend. The European artificed production of the desires, needs, wants of Africans everywhere — and this is no less true of the Black-on-Black criminal — is one and the same thing as European construction of African social relations.

Just as the behavior of the "normal" individual cannot be adequately explained in terms of drives, lacks, ... either can the behavior of neurotics, perverts, psychotics, and Black-on-Black criminals. A person eats for many reasons other than hunger, or a lack or need for certain nutrients. The more important forms of human behavior are not merely instigated by needs to reduce or satisfy some *pre*existing intrinsic drive. They are conditionally motivated and organized by extrinsically produced and defined incentives or enticements. As the social and material incentives manufactured by White America are invented by its makers, so are African American desires and their related behaviors, be they criminal or otherwise.

What many African Americans, including Black-on-Black criminals desire most are those things manufactured, owned, controlled, and sold by their White oppressors. African Americans rarely *want* or *value* anything else. The White American ruling class devalues what it does not own or control, and invests with inflated value what it does own or control, thereby provoking possessive/obsessive desires in the deprived groups it dominates. It sets the material and social prices to be paid for obtaining what it owns, controls and/or offers for sale. Through its manipulation of production and prices it seeks to manipulate the social conditions and organization (as well as disorganization) of the behavior, perception and consciousness of those who seek to acquire what it produces. Its production methods and organization sustain the status quo and the system of values and social relations which support its hegemony.

Desiring Production and Regulation of Social Relations

To whom and to what the socialized individual relates, how he relates to them, his feelings (or lack thereof) toward them, are related to, if not determined by, a matrix of extrinsically machinated desires, needs, and wants. That is, the social field in which the individual is immersed is invested with desire. For example, the individual who is addicted to "crack" moves in a field of social relations, perceptions, feelings, and attitudes invested with and colored by his addictive desires. Those persons, objects, and situations which populate his social sphere of activity are defined by his obsessive desires; and he relates to them in accordance with such desires. A change in his addictive pursuits would bring about a concomitant change in the nature and quality of his social relations, attitudes and behavior. The *crack*-selling establishment is dependent on his investing his social relations with his addictive desires. That establishment's manipulation of his addictive desires and behaviors is paralleled by its simultaneous manipulation of his field of social relations, feelings, and attitudes. The organization of the crack addict's addictive desires by the crack-selling establishment maintains that establishment's organizational infrastructure. Without the addict's desire it would not exist.

The production of African American desire by the European manufacturing of that desire not only maintains and reproduces the European productive and social establishment, and structures Black/White race relations: it also maintains, reproduces, and structures African American inter-communal, intra-communal, interpersonal attitudes and relations. Just as the "crack" addict values and devalues persons relative to his addiction, to his desire to satisfy his artificial hunger, so does the Black-on-Black criminal, addicted to artificial hungers, devalue other Blacks if by such devaluation he may satisfy his addiction to White American products.

The Black-on-Black criminal is one whose desires have been so organized by the White American system of production and its correlated social order that he, much like his bourgeois law-abiding counterparts, views his own people as mere objects and instruments for his fulfillment. Unlike his bourgeois counterparts, he is willing to engage in personally administered violence, to relate to and react violently with his people in order to satisfy his White American created fantasies. As his desires are organized by the White American social order, so is his violence.

The commercial activation of desire beyond certain critical levels can and does negate other more positive feelings such as empathy, sympathy, and love. Intense, frustrated, egocentric desire and love cannot co-exist. *Under the pressure of intense desire love is transformed into addiction.* Addiction means the misuse and abuse of the other and of the self.

The White American-owned and -controlled market economy and its concomitant social order not only instigates and organizes desires; they frustrate them as well. As the chief frustrator of the desires it provokes, the American racial/class system also instigates violence — one of the byproducts of frustration. The American culture is preoccupied with the creation and production of frustrated desire and need. These are over-determined and overproduced. However, to maintain its class and power structure, its racial hierarchy, along with the status symbols pertaining thereunto, the fulfillment of establishment-instigated desires and needs must be withheld from many constituents of American society. Artificial scarcities must be maintained in the face of overproduction and abundance. The unfulfilled must be made to feel unworthy and unblessed. They must be incapacitated, disabled, barred from employment, robbed of appropriate recompense for their labor, excluded from facilitating social interaction and relations, if they are to be kept in "their place."

The racial/class hierarchy in America is maintained through the White American maintenance of large discrepancies between the objects of desire they produce and the means by which they are obtained. Gross imbalances between means and ends, between expectations and the possibilities of their fulfillment, are endemic to American society. It does little, if anything, to prepare its citizens to fulfill the expectations it socializes into them, or to provide them with wholesome and affordable means of self-fulfillment.

Desire, if intense enough, often operates against "common sense," practical logic, ethical values, personal standards, and self-preservation. Under the influence of pervasive desire, the subject is compelled not to act in terms of the *ought to be,* on *doing the right thing,* or of taking the long-term view of the consequences of short-term behavior. Benefit/cost analyses are warped, suspended, or ignored. This implies that under the aegis of dominant class- or group-produced desires and values — desires and values formulated to further ruling class interests — subordinate interests or groups are prone to act in direct opposition of their very interests. By investing their material and mental resources and energies in accord with the ruling group's production and social organizational strategies, subordinate groups ally themselves with groups or classes whose interests and ideologies, given their objective circumstances, they should oppose to the death. Under the sway of ruling class production, marketing strategies, and the related social formations, values, and ideologies, the subordinate classes purchase their bondage with their own coins.

Desire and the Creation of Black-on-Black Criminality

According to Walker and Heyns, "The greater and more valued the reward, the oftener it is achieved through conforming behavior, the more conformist the behavior is likely to become, the more likely it is to become a generalized way of behaving in new situations. The person need not be aware of these effects."[22] This generalization is essentially a specific restatement of the central thesis of learning theory, i.e., that behavior is determined by its consequences; that the likelihood of a particular set of responses is increased if the occurrence of those responses are followed by a reinforcer or reward. The more consistently a targeted behavior is followed by a reward, the more likely the behavior is to recur. In essence, Walker and Heyns imply that a society is more likely to increase the conformity

---

[22] Walker, E. & Heyns, R. *An Anatomy of Conformity.* New Jersey: Prentice Hall, 1962.

behavior (e.g., law abiding behavior) of its constituents by consistently rewarding that behavior, by making it possible for the conformist to obtain desired objectives, by punishing or not rewarding nonconformist behavior, and/or by making it possible for the conformist to avoid relatively painful alternatives. Conversely, a society increases the nonconformity behavior (e.g., criminal behavior) of its constituents by making it socially possible for such behavior to occur by consistently rewarding that behavior. That is, by making it possible for the nonconformist to obtain desired objectives; by punishing or not rewarding conformist behavior; and by making it possible for the nonconformist to avoid relatively painful alternatives.

Through *differential reinforcement* and *punishment* (e.g., racial discrimination practices), a society can simultaneously encourage apparent law-abidingness in one group and criminality in another. This is the case in American society relative to its White American and Black American sub-populations.

In the United States of America, African Americans are hypocritically proffered the same socially valued (positive) incentives for expressing the same conformity behavior and attributes as European Americans. However, due to racial discrimination African Americans are many times not only denied the same rewards for exhibiting the same conformity behavior and attitudes as do European Americans but are punished for doing so. In many instances, a promised or expected positive incentive is withheld after the behavior for which it was to be a reward is expressed. Consequently, the formerly positive incentive may come to be perceived as a *negative incentive* by the deluded party. A negative incentive refers to an object[*ive*] or circumstance away from which behavior is directed. This racist approach for conditioning conformist behavior is prevalent in American society and has the effect of increasing apparent social conformity among White Americans and decreasing relative social conformity among Black Americans. Furthermore, racial discrimination in the United States effectively restricts the opportunities, facilities, and other conditions for learning certain conformity or rewarding behavior among African Americans relative to Europeans, thereby restricting the number of African Americans who learn such behavior. This situation effectively increases the number or percentage of African Americans who have not learned, and who therefore exhibit certain socially unacceptable behavior. Thus, the racial dimension of the relative percentage of certain conformity versus nonconformity behavior per Black or White American subgroup tend to remain relatively the same even if they both receive the same reward for the same conformity behavior. In fact, under such circumstances the percentages would tend to remain relatively the same even if the Blacks were relatively better rewarded for exhibiting the same conformity behavior as Whites.

Moreover, the American market economy is huge and "blind." It freely and without question exchanges its socially manufactured products for monies — regardless of how such monies were obtained by the purchaser. The American market economy was and is built and sustained by the blood-monies of thieves, crooks, and murders. When such denizens of criminality are permitted to obtain self-esteem, self-indulgence, social adulation, respectability, influence, power and prestige, or at least purchase or obtain with monies earned by nonconformity (law-breaking) behavior the same goods and services that are extended to the "legitimately rich and famous," then, such behavior is rewarded and therefore encouraged by the American market economy.

White America, through its racist practices as described above, effectively increases the relative percentage of Black Americans who must exhibit nonconformity or criminal behavior, and in addition, rewards them for exhibiting that behavior by permitting them to purchase self-esteem, self-indulgence, social acceptance and respectability to obtain the emblems, status symbols, and indulgences associated with the rich and famous. Hence, White America can be said to unequivocally reward, and thereby encourage criminality in the African American community. When Black-on-Black criminals, catalyzed by White racism in America can purchase White American-owned, controlled and valuated social products with their monies earned more easily by slaughtering or maliciously injuring or destroying the African American community than by respecting and enhancing it, then the blame for such slaughter and destruction must be placed squarely on the White/European American community. The White American community, via its racist infrastructure and traditions, must bear full responsibility for both creating or encouraging a significant amount of Black-on-Black criminality and other forms of maladaptive behavior, by surreptitiously rewarding and profiting from it. The monies earned from Black-on-Black crime almost invariably and immediately ends-up in White American hands.

White-on-Black vs. Black-on-Black Criminality

It is difficult for racist White Americans to emotionally comprehend White-on-Black violence "truly criminal." This is the major reason why *White-on-Black* criminals are, relatively speaking, rarely arrested, indicted, convicted, or *if* convicted, are given light sentences. Conversely, *Black-on-White* criminality is relatively swiftly and severely punished. Moreover, Black-on-Black crime, regardless of its severity, if contained in the Black ghettos and if perceived as not threatening the safety, security, peace, and profits of the White American community, is generally not emotionally perceived in the same way, or investigated and prosecuted with the same vigor as is *White-on-White* crime. Blacks killing and criminally assaulting each other is taken as a matter *of course*, if not with a morbid sense of self-congratulatory moral superiority by White Americans. Such behavior on the part of Blacks helps to justify White racist practices and assuage related White guilt. Unfortunately, such White American prosecutorial practices, attitudes and feelings do little to inhibit, if not actually encourage and subtly reward, Black-on-Black criminality. Given the sociohistorical and contemporaneous racist functional structure of the American production system and its related social order, the White American community must accept the fact that it profits psychologically and materially from White-on-Black violence and domination, and from the death and damnation of the victims of Black-on-Black violence committed under the impetus of desires and needs artificially evoked by the White American economic hegemony.

The Choice

The White American community controls the means by which African American social and material desires and needs are created, stimulated, and more often than not, severely frustrated. Such frustration in turn leads to various types of *mal*adaptive behavior, including Black-on-Black violence. Overall, the outcome of this situation is sociopsychologically and materially profitable for the White American community and is therefore unlikely to be changed by that community. Consequently, if the African American community is not to be sacrificed to White American lust, vanity and greed — if it is not to self-annihilate — it must make three compelling and imminent choices. It either must:

- seize ownership and control of the means of production or influence them in ways such that it can satisfy the stimulated desires and needs of its members;
- radically modify the tastes, desires, values, and needs of its members such that their vain pursuit of them will not underwrite their own oppression or self-destruction;
- or radically transform the American production and value systems, social order, and replace them by a new, fairer (*blacker*), humane social and economic order.

9

DREAMS WITHOUT MEANS

"I want so many things, it drives me crazy
... money is life!"

— LORRAINE HANSBURY
A Raisin In The Sun

The Black-on-Black Criminal as Conspicuous Consumer

THE BLACK-ON-BLACK violent criminal is no rebel. He is no revolutionary. He is the consummate conformist, the pre-eminent *bourgeois gentilhomme.* He is the outlaw who kills to break the silence, to make visible his invisibility, to make something out of the nothingness of his existence. He will be noticed. He will be heard. He will be catered to.

All he needs are the symbols, the emblems of power — the magic wands, sacred gems, golden pendants and rings, majestic robes and coiffure, chariots and retinue, the royal scents and perfumes, the treasury — and the will to follow the route of all would-be kings and pretenders, to violently acquire them and even more violently to increase and defend them.

The Black-on-Black violent criminal, possessed by the intro-jected spirit of his White racist fathers, is host to the same internalized insatiable appetitive cravings, material adornments,

135

and addictive status hunger as are the White racists who bastardized him. Like them, he pays unresisting obeisance to only one regent — the fulfillment of his ever expanding rapacious desires. However, disinherited of his White racist father's powers and means, and consequently restricted in his choice of methods and victims, he can only scavenge the leavings of his violated mind and *body* and those of his biological and affinal mothers, fathers, sisters, brothers, sons and daughters. And even the relatively meager and ephemeral returns violently wrested from the African community by the Black-on-Black criminal through the use of terror, abuse and the pushing of various addictions, are brought to the storehouses of his White fathers and exchanged for overpriced trinkets, musical playthings, adult toys, fool's gold, momentary fads and a variety of other "psycho-lollipops."

An outsider, the Black-on-Black criminal is attracted to outward appearances, consumption patterns, and the symbolic appurtenances of his White racist models. He wants what they have; the symbols of their power and status, that which make him appear important, feared, and respected. He equates form, appearance, conspicuous consumption, and ostentatious material possessions with substance; illusory appearance with concrete reality. Unlike his murderous White racist models who transform their application of violence into "legitimate" productive and reproductive "real estate," "equity," technology, wealth and sociopolitically rationalized power, the Black-on-Black criminal, all appetite, uninterested and untutored in the ways of transformation, trades the blood of his fellow victims for an empty charade — a childish, savage caricature of his White racist fathers. He is the paradigm of racism in Black face, the supreme White racist and supremacist! He foolishly thinks the capacity to do violence "makes" him a man — like "the man." He thinks the wearing of gaudy rings and the driving of flashy cars "makes" him "somebody." Thus the Black criminal, while the consummate consumer, is rarely an investor. A renter, he rarely owns. A sensation, never a power. He is ever the conduit and the transfer agent; never the repository. He must chronically look for and fleece new victims. He continues until violence, death, imprisonment, old age, or some "born again" religious addiction ends his predatory existence.

Desire and the Black-on-Black Criminal

Desire is the *elan vital,* the lifeblood, the psychoanatomical infrastructure of the imperialistic White racist economic/psycho-political system. Insatiable, nymphomaniacal desire, and the endemically compulsive and fruitless intercourse required to maintain its functionality, are the fuels which energize and motivate its behavioral organization, the universal joints which coordinate, control, and regulate the functional workings of its constituent parts. The production of desire and the manufac-turing of accessory insatiable needs, envies, unrequitable alienation, invidious comparisons, and relative feelings of deprivation, are the primary and quintessential cultural activities upon which all else depends. Philip Slater, unerringly defines the White American economic character when he in his book, *The Pursuit of Loneliness*, asserts that:

> The mass media are always telling us to satisfy our emotional needs with material products — particularly through, oral consumption. Our economy depends upon our willingness to turn to things rather than people for gratification — to symbols rather than our bodies. The gross national product will reach its highest point when a material object can be interpolated between every itch, and its scratch.

He also states that:

> Hunger, thirst, and sexual desire in pure form can be slaked, but the desire for a body type that was invented by cartoonists cannot. Neither can the desire for fame, power, or wealth. These are invidious needs; they are satisfied only in relation to the deprivation of others. Furthermore, they're purely symbolic and hence have no endpoint. A man hooked on fame or power will never stop striving because there is no way to gratify a desire with a symbol.[23]

As long as the economy and ancillary systems can provide the wherewithal to come within "striking" distance of attaining

---

[23] Slater, Philip. *The Pursuit of Loneliness: American Culture at the Breaking Point.* Rev. ed. Boston: Beacon Press, 1976.

the "American dream" for some, sustain the *hope* of attaining it for others by "legitimate" means, and provide for the rationalized, moralized, narcotized resignation of the rest who are not even permitted to run in the mainstream rat-race, the system works, and its peace, law and order, maintained. The manufacture of invidious needs and desires and selling bogus satisfactions serve their insidious function. For the Black-on-Black criminal — restricted to his ghettos, bereft of afrocentrically acculturated active interests, aims, values, or goals which reach beyond the immediate concerns of *his* own life, shorn of a stable matrix of Afrocentric culturally-based historical and long-range interests, values, and emotional involvements as the result of having received a thorough White racist miseducation for consumption and endless servitude — these "invidious" needs and desires are all the more intense. Uninhibited by a self-serving introjected White racist "conscience" or superego, unacculturated by an Afrocentric identity, and schooled in violence by overexposure to a violent existence, the Black-on-Black criminal is puppeted unmercifully by his White racist manufactured desires and passions. He is committed to attain the icons emblematic of having actualized the "dream," having captured the "golden fleece," and having achieved some "eminence" by the criminal means so readily at his disposal.

Needs, Wants and Desires

The White American economic system and the global White supremacist economic system depend on the unrestrained African American and worldwide African impulse to consume gluttonously all the items manufactured by Whites or other ethnic groups, regardless of value or utility. These economic systems depend on African peoples defining and evaluating themselves in terms of their consumption of European or other foreign-made goods; not as producers for their own utilitarian and other needs, and the consummatory needs of other peoples. In his assigned role as consumer *par excellence*, and not as producer, the African is motivated to value consumption above all other activities. He is tantalized by the European marketing system to consume indiscriminately and to perceive the capacity to consume, to *display* luxurious adornments, and engage in a caricature the lifestyles of the "rich and famous" as the most veridical measure of human worth, power and prestige. This illusion of "somebodi-ness" and worth attained via consumption and conspicuous display without the concomitant "ownership of the means of production," without the sociopolitical power and organization to attain such ownership, requires that an impulsive-compulsive orientation toward monetary profligacy and debauchery be introjected at the center of the African personality. One man's profligacy and debauchery are the sources of another man's wealth and power and psychopolitical hegemony. The dissolute African American, without the support or ownership of, or compelling interest in developing the means of producing for his own consummatory proclivities, without having access to workable "legitimate" strategies for acquiring those means, is perfectly "set up" to be pushed into criminal activities in order to assuage his artificially induced desires.

The irrational economy of White America, based as it is on irrational consumption, requires a high level of impulsivity and economic stupidity in its population; all the more in its lower classes and subordinated African American population. It requires a subordinate population molded and motivated by external, White American-instigated desires and images. The White American racist commercialization of life, consciousness, and values are the sources of White racist hegemonic power and dominance. The alleged inability of many African Americans to delay gratification; their tendency to compulsively invest vast sums of money and onerous credit in ephemeral, faddish symbols and icons, flashy styles of life; to achieve identity through conspicuous consumption and pursue validation through image management rather than substance; and to pursue these at whatever cost to self and community; is an economic and political necessity for maintaining White American dominance and African American subordination.

Whether these costs include Black-on-Black predatory criminality matters little to the dominant White American community so long as that criminality is contained within the confines of the African American community, provides profits for White criminal overlords and White so-called business establishments, as well as provide employment for the White American constabulary, criminal justice establishment, and provides cannon fodder for the White American rationalization of the oppression of African peoples. The essence of the White

American hegemonic system is that of a pecking order of vampires, each level sucking to the point of death the blood of the ranks below it. Criminality is perceived as a threat to this sequence of "law and order" when a lower rank "gets out of line," pecks and sucks above its level, or threatens to disrupt the coordinated and smooth flow of blood into the supersaturated blood banks of those at the top of the vampiristic hierarchy.

Adornment and Black-on-Black Criminality

The Black-on-Black predatory criminal like many other African Americans, but to a more intense and ungoverned degree, is beguiled into the vain and destructive pursuit of impressionistic personal adornments and public lifestyles. This is often the result of having been insulted by White Americans and Europeans. He struggles by pecuniary means to overcome, to deny or divert personal and public attention away from his eurocentrically depreciated African body, culture, heritage, history and future. He wants to be seen as an exception to the "rest of those niggers." He wants to break through his invisibility into the consciousness of others, to stand out, to symbolize his having through willfulness, assertiveness and cunning escaped his assigned place and image in the eurocentrically determined socioeconomic and racialist order. Through adornment, his jewels, expensive junk, he lifts himself up and enhances his self-feelings. He "ranks" others as he himself is ranked. According to Simmel, in *The Sociology of Georg Simmel*:

> Adornment is the egoistic element as such: it singles out its wearer, whose self-feeling it embodies and increases at the cost of others (for, the same adornment of all would no longer adorn the individual). But at the same time, adornment is altruistic: its pleasure is designed for others, since its owner can enjoy it only in so far as he mirrors himself in them; he renders the adornment valuable only through the reflection of this gift of his.[24]

Simmel further intimates that:

---

[24] Wolff. R. *The Sociology of George Simmel.* New York: Macmillan, 1950.

...the aesthetic phenomenon of adornment indicates a point within sociological interactions — the arena of man's being-for-himself and being for-the-other — where these two opposite directions are mutually dependent as ends and means.[25]

Through exaggerated or conspicuous consumption, through gaudily bejewelled fingers, gold-covered teeth, outsized clothes, overpriced sneakers, expensive cars of the lower class, or the buttoned down tailoring of the middle class, the diminished African American personality is transformed, intensified and amplified, and radiates beyond its limitations to intrude into the world of others who would ignore or summarily dismiss it. His sphere of influence broadens, carrying others along in its wake.

It is through his dressed ostentatiousness, his conspicuous consumption that the African American, offended by White racism, fights back. Consumption and display are his weapons of choice, which, as paltry substitutes for substantial revolutionary preparation and action, have been selected to defy the incursions by and restraints of his enemies. If he cannot defeat them, unbalance them, neutralize them, perhaps seduce or convert them, he can at the very least, gain their begrudging and envious attention. He achieves reality and higher social standing through getting the attention of the other, particularly the other who would ignore, dismiss or demote him. Only when he is "seen" by those Europeans who have insulted him, when he can impress them with his buying power, get the envious attention of the "rest of the niggers," does he come into being, does he become "somebody."

Through the monetary worth of his possessions, his jewels, clothes, cars, houses, rents, he, in a relatively safe way, compensates for the worthlessness of being Black in America. He, the worth of his possessions, and the modish arrangement of his attire, are one. The worth of the one speaks of the worthiness of the other. Together they glaringly refute the would-be put-downs of others, shields him against, and makes him impervious to, the slings and arrows of others. To have is to be.

---

[25] Ibid.

To have beyond necessity, to have in excess, is to be larger than one's origins, to rise above one's station and speak for oneself, to make one's own statement and be heard. The eurocentrically negated African image is dissolved in the universality and universal language of coveted objects, "looks," modes of consumption and privileges. Jewelry and the capacity to consume the "latest", the newest, moves the negated African American beyond the individual, the merely ethnic, into the supra-individual and supra-ethnic. He is, though individually unique, transpersonalized and internationalized, no longer a stereotypical stand-in for an outcast group of people. Yet, at bottom it is all illusion — a charade. For expensive accouterments and conspicuous consumption are merely the epiphenomena of power, not defensive weapons for African peoples against European military assault; they are not insurance policies against oppression by other peoples, or against insidious diseases and self-destructive impulses. Unsupported by power — ownership of land, resources, production and distribution facilities, a brain trust, an army — a nation of individual consumers is doomed to continued subordination, exploitation and ultimate annihilation. If the possession of dead, inanimate objects becomes the highest priority of such a nation of individuals — individuals who own nothing to speak of, who can only sell their labor to a limited and scandalously underpaid extent, who do not own themselves or their appetites — then, many in that conglomerate barrel of crabs will prey on each other to possess them.

The acquisitive African American motivated by insult, is placed in the position, as the result of believing the lie that one can compensate for the lack of fundamental powers and capacities and for personal and collective vulnerabilities by purchasing at too high a price, at the cost of self-immolation, the manufacture of the ones who insulted him in the first place. To be African in America is to vainly attempt to rise above insult by subsidizing and enhancing the power of the insulter — the European/White American community. Stuffed to the gills with eurocentrically created desires for things insubstantial, ephemeral and merely symbolic, yet denied "legitimate" means of satisfying those desires, the Black-on-Black criminal introjectedly chooses to engage in the endless pursuit of those things at the price of jeopardizing the minds, bodies, souls and spirits of his people, of his children, himself, to the crass benefit of those who are worthy only of his contempt.

In sum, the commercial role of the African American in the United States, and the African in general, is that of producer of raw materials, cheap labor, and consumer of White American and European-produced goods and services. It is his role as consumer and how it relates to his criminality that concerns us here. To play his role as consumer to the hilt while destroying himself and others in the process requires that the African personality contain certain operative characteristics. It requires a distortion of values through their commercialization, as well as the continuous creation of desire and change of tastes by those who own the means of satisfying those created desires and tastes — the European economic establishment.

As a consumer of European or non-African produced necessities, luxuries, and "junk," the African American must not be able to differentiate between the three, and if so, see the latter as fulfilling what amounts to a primary need in his personality. He was and is prepared for his commercial role by his White American oppressor/conditioner through the impairment of his critical faculties, the heightening of his commercial suggestibility, appetites, emotionality, and impulsivity. While he may share these characteristics with the rest of the consumer population, his problems lie in the fact that the society which conditions him for consumption, does not condition him to provide for the legitimate satiation of his artificially created appetitive needs. There are no independent means of providing him with the earned income to buy what he wants, or providing him with the values and abilities to delay gratification by means of which he could constrain his consummatory desires until he is able to "legitimately" fulfill them.

In order to maximize its profits from the African American community, and to keep its markets open to its optimal exploitation, the White American community destroys and impairs the growth and development of an indigenous African American economy by a variety of means. The appetite of the individual African American must be so stimulated and shaped that he is willing to sacrifice the economic future of his community for immediate gratification. This requires that he be educated into a certain fundamental stupidity; be gullible to commercial lies; be taken in by false, illogical images and symbols; that he be given over to impulsiveness; that he suffers lack of judgment, stabilizing values and identity. He must become what he consumes, and the more he consumes the more he becomes "somebody." He must define his self-realization in terms of rapacious consumption and monetary worth. He must lose self-control and self-directedness. His locus of control must be external and other-directed, rather than internally controlled and self-directed. His appetitive desires and goals must be dictated by others; his opinion of himself unduly influenced by the opinions of others. He must experience such an intense existential loneliness and alienation that he vainly seeks to buy the respect, attention, friendship, and love of others to the detriment of his own, his family's (not to mention his community's) economic security, power, and psychosocial health.

As the perfect consumer "fall guy," the African American consumer must be possessed by a "heteronomous" superego which, instead of demanding that he behave in an ethically "good" way, according to reason, foresight, and sound moral principles for the benefit of his community, demands that he behave in accordance to what is expected by peer groups, momentary and faddish demands and images created by advertising.[26] What is "in" is right. His Afrocentric superego or conscience — based on self-knowledge, knowledge of African culture and history; a deep, analogous, objective analysis of African and European culture; a clear set of self-preserving and self-enhancing goals founded on an African identity and self-love — must be replaced by a self-serving Eurocentric, White American, materialistic, cultural superego or conscience. The possessive White American conscience must control the objects of African people's love and loyalty and their personal obligatory objectives. Values, aims, goals, interests, emotional commitments, love and friendships must be short-term or shallow; short of tolerance and patience; cognition characterized by concreteness, passivity, reactionary immediateness, emotionality, egocentricity; by a relative lack of long-range planning, lack of capacity for active, detailed concentration, reflectiveness, abstraction and conceptualization. His world must be discontinuous, inconstant,

---

[26] Fenichel, Otto. *The Psychoanalytical Theory of Neurosis.* New York: W.W. Norton, 1945.

uncertain, sensuous, opportunistic, full of temptations and fragmented impressions. Not only must he be dominated by wishful thinking, the immediately impressive, the striking, the colorful, the exciting, the forcefully presented, the emotionally stirring, the romantic, and the phantasmagorical, but these orientations must be utilized as substitutes for facts, relevant knowledge and critical analysis.[27] In other words, the ideal African American consumer must be essentially impulsive and hysterical.

Relatively speaking, the above characterizations and orientations are generally neutralized, attenuated, sublimated, or inhibited in the American White and Black upper- and middle-classes (though measurably less so for the Black classes) by their capacity to materially and socially meet their appetitive demands or by their conditioning to play their socioeconomic roles as rulers and managers. Relative self-control and related forms of thinking, behavioral and emotional control, are required of the controllers and managers of others. This requires that external controls, values, and other supposed factors be internalized, rationalized, and claimed as one's own, and the belief that in a stable world one's political needs, desires and wishes will be eventually satisfied, and that the means for their satisfaction are available, or will be, in a reasonable period of time. The middle class is a class of *self-control* — a delusion; but an effective one nevertheless. Its locus of control is internal, and its introjected superego (or conscience) relatively effective. This is also the case for the bulk of the "law-abiding" lower- and working-classes, whose "hope for a better tomorrow," fear of punishment, religiosity, or acceptance of their condition and status they see as cosmically or karmically their due.

However, there is a class of people who, lacking "appropriate" values and countervalues, whose behavior is basically reactionary because their role is to be other-controlled by means of extrinsically manipulated rewards and punishments, and to whom the "legitimate" gates of opportunity are closed, may engage in criminal behavior. This class includes the Black-on-Black violent criminal.

---

[27] Shapiro, David. *Neurotic Styles.* New York: Basic Books, 1965.

Hence, lacking or suffering from relatively weak internal restraints the Black-on-Black violent criminal feels "impelled" by his desires for stimulation, excitement and need satisfaction, as well as by the attractiveness of objects and opportunity, to engage in antisocial behavior. Feeling the need to express and demonstrate his manhood, he does so by the only means his White American conditioned shortsightedness presents to him — interpersonal violence and exploitation. Robbed of an affirming racial and personal identity and of pre-occupying positive cultural and familial goals by a greedy, criminal, White American economic establishment, he claims the full manhood and independence denied him by instrumentally utilizing violence as a means to attain those status symbols emblematic of his doubtful masculinity and autonomy. As intimated above, much of Black-on-Black violence, robbery, thievery, assault, stealing, and others, are motivated and sustained by Black males seeking to obtain or purchase these objects they have been conditioned to think of as important to their *status* and high self-regard, or to gain narcotic euphoriants and analgesics in order deal with the frustration of not having attained them, or as adjuncts to their attainment.

Shorn of an affirming identity so that he may assume any identity and correlated behavioral tendency imposed on him by the dominant White supremacist establishment, the Black-on-Black criminal may turn to crime and violence in order to gain a commercialized identity and fulfill the need of the dominant establishment to perceive him and the African American community as criminal in character. Since the things he will steal, rob, or kill for, change over time (the goals of his criminality are most often influenced by current fads and crazes) he is made to appear to be chronically, innately, and incorrigibly criminal by a White American establishment, which just as chronically and incorrigibly bars his way to positive self-actualization. The Black-on-Black violent criminal only expresses to an extreme degree, the sickness of the whole African American community, for he is continuous with it. The relative "noncriminality" and "law-abidingness" of the vast majority of the African American community is not due so much to their moral superiority, (as is no more the case for the White American community), better judgment or "family backgrounds." Rather it is due, in large part, to their introjection of a self-serving White American religious conscience, of White American ethical and cultural values, and more important — their desperate acceptance of an alien identity. For this acceptance they have been, and are, materially and socially rewarded (*the poorer ones will be rewarded in Heaven*) and have been permitted, unlike their criminal relatives, to purchase or to buy on credit the trinkets, condescending tolerance and attention of their White American or European counterparts. For this, they sell their souls, sell-out their community, and the future of their race. For this, they are even more criminal than their thieving, violent brothers.

The Self-Alienated Black Body

The psychopathological concern with body adornments is derivative of severe self-alienation and is indicative of intensely painful conflicts between the ego and the body. By psychological concern with *adornment* we refer to the situation where the individual is willing to use illegal or criminal means in order to obtain very expensive, luxurious, or overpriced faddish, usually gaudy, social status symbols. These illegal means include the willingness on his part to sell addictive or self-destructive substances, and willingness to personally rob, viciously assault, or murder, another person. Pathological concern may also include the instance wherein the desire to purchase such adornments is so intense and self-centered that the individual may sacrifice familial responsibilities, and sacrifice long-term personal, educational, communal, cultural and other more productive, worthwhile interests in order to obtain them. This type of concern, additionally, may include the feelings of insignificance, invisibility, powerlessness, unworthiness, isolation, depression, inferiority, and other self-negating feelings when the individual is unable to obtain certain body adornments.

By adorning his body with various and unusual combinations of cultural or subcultural status symbols, the individual may hope to project his self-image in ways which influence his consciousness and behavior and in ways he considers advantageous and/or pleasing to himself and others. The projected personal/social image hopefully created by his body adornment, is designed to mobilize a particular type of response from others, to incite a variety of reactions such as deference, admiration, envy, acceptance, or fear. When derivative of rather severe self-alienation or of powerful though unconscious conflicts, the manipulative projection of an image through body adornments implies that the body so adorned is being utilized as an object, as an instrument, as a prop to support a staged performance.

Under conditions of deep self-alienation, where the individual feels compelled by very painful or perhaps life-threatening pressures to reject his real self — and along with it his natural body, his use of an overdressed facade, or his adoption of a costumed role as a means of achieving the social acceptance of peers and of achieving visibility, prestige and identity — thus denotes the presence of a split between his body and soul. This further implies that the individual is utilizing the adornment of his body as an instrument of denial and repression of his real self and of some important aspects of reality. Self-alienated adornment of the body implies that the individual may intensely dislike his natural body or may perceive it as the only really acceptable and lovable characteristic he possesses. His beautifully adorned body may be used under such circumstances to veneer what he unconsciously perceives as an untidy, ugly inner-reality.

According to Alexander Lowen:

> ...identification with the body [is] the foundation upon which the personal life is erected. ..."mental health" refers to the condition where image and reality coincide. A healthy person has an image of himself that agrees with the way that his body looks and feels.[28]

When the individual has experienced his body as a source of shame, degradation, painful social rejection and negative discrimination; when he perceives it in its natural state as the enemy of his personal social successes, he can maintain an identification with his body which is at best, tenuously ambivalent, or at worst, nonexistent (as in some cases of schizophrenia). In the latter case he may become disembodied and depersonalized, feelings symptomatic of a schizoid existence.

> ...the schizoid individual knows he has a body and is, therefore, oriented in time and space. But since his ego is not identified

---

[28] Lowen, A. *The Betrayal of the Body*. New York: Collier Books, 1967.

with his body and does not perceive it in an alive way, he feels unrelated to the way he feels about himself. This conflict does not exist in a healthy person whose ego is identified with his body and in whom the knowledge of his identity stems from feelings of the body.[29]

When the individual, for any number reasons, cannot accept his body, he loses vital, honest contact with it and in turn loses vital accurate contacts with reality. The body may become objectified and a source of counterfeit identity. The objectification of the body, the loss of its oneness with the mind, motivates the disembodied individual to replace it with a confected personal/body image. Such a confected self-image is utilized not only to maintain denial, but is utilized as the only source of alienated, illusory feelings of aliveness, pleasure, power, competence, satisfaction, and accomplishment.

Thus, vicious circles are established. The more the self-alienated individual becomes addicted to good or ecstatic feelings attained through rejection of his real self, certain aspects of reality, the objectification of his body, the operational construction of his counterfeit personal/body image, the more he feels compelled to acquire the adornments which makes such feelings possible. The more the adorned body image he projects becomes the source of positive self-feelings and self-regard, the more he intends to inflate that body image through the acquisition of adornments. The more he inflates his image in his own eyes, the more he blinds himself to reality and the more he detaches himself from his commonsense and good judgement. The more he inflates and identifies with his confected body image, the more he loses a sense of his personal humanity, the more he becomes an abstraction. The more he becomes an embellished body image, a gaudy abstraction, the more he perceives others as mere images, abstractions, and non-persons.

The perceptions of others as animated effigies, combined with the compellingly addictive need to acquire the adornments thought necessary to maintain an alienated self-image — yet unbuttressed by the legitimate means of their acquisition — may, under certain circumstances, move the individual to acquire them

---

[29] Ibid.

by destructive or violent means. These are some of the conditions under which Black-on-Black violence and criminality are produced, particularly among young African American males.

Enslavement and the continued exploitation of Africans in America and the world-over by White America and Europeans require that Africans be perceived by Europeans as stereotypical images and abstractions. The efficient and unconscionable manipulative exploitation of African people by Europeans, requires that Africans perceive themselves as images and abstractions and be motivated by image management rather than by their reality-based feelings, desires and needs. Forced to conform to or reactionarily deny European projected images of themselves, many Africans are moved to lose a sense of themselves, their feelings of identity and connection with reality and their bodies. In conjunction with these losses Africans also surrender the capacity to realistically perceive the Europeans for what they are in reality. They therefore become susceptible to being manipulated self-destructively by the false image projected by their White oppressors.

The alienation of the African from his body began with his alienation from his land, his culture, his Gods, followed by his alienation from his manhood and the expropriation of the fruits of his labors. His self-alienation began when others perceived him as alien, as a body, as object, instrument, "field hand," "laborer," "boy," "buck," "nigger...." The objectification of his body began when the others used his body as instrument, object, asset.

The severely self-alienated African then began to perceive his own body as instrument, as object, as tool. He and it became not the same. His body has never been his. From the beginning it has always belonged to someone else. He can only borrow it, rent it out, share-crop it, or dress it up like a kewpie-doll. It's his wind-up toy. He winds it up and watches it work. It's for show, to be used to seduce. He dresses it up to attract attention to it and simultaneously to detract attention away from it. It is the source of his shame and of his pride.

Though trapped in it he has lost touch with it, and having lost touch with it he lost touch with himself and the world — lost touch with his feelings and humanity. These can only be reclaimed, along with his liberation, when he reclaims his African body and African self. For they are one and the same.

Exportation and Importation of Crime and Criminality

We should note that Western Europe suffered grievously from banditry, gangs of knights errant, criminal syndicates, highwaymen, knaves, vagrants, class tensions and social dislocations, murder and mayhem in its royal houses and common hovels — outlawry of various descriptions — for centuries prior to its discovery, conquest, enslavement, decimation, and colonization of non-European populations. An argument can be made that the latter activities relative to non-European populations permitted Western Europe to "export" its troublemakers and criminals, and to "legitimize" the expression of their criminality and homicidal habits on "savage" populations.

Consequently, Western Europe was able to reduce, over time, its class, religious, political and other tensions and criminality within its own realms by "exporting" them to its colonies. In the colonies, what would have been defined as the most outrageous criminality in Western Europe was sanctioned by royal decree or White power and thereby legitimized. In addition to its exportation of crime and criminality — its proportional reduction of criminality and tensions within its borders — Western Europe imported the wealth of its captive populations and lands and thereby gained the relative advantages of material prosperity, power, and industrialization which permitted it to better clothe, feed and shelter large portions of its population. By these and other means, it was able to reduce or change the quality of crime within its societies. After their initial criminal depredations, a similar path to relative "noncriminality" was followed by the Whites who dominated its colonies.

Thus, through wars of colonization, slavery, and other warlike acts of *pacification* of natives and through the legitimization of their economic organization and domination of the resources of their decimated or colonized populations, Europeans exported, legitimized and hid their criminality from themselves. They eventually came to perceive themselves as inherently virtuous and law-abiding by comparison. They could only see the criminality in the faces and characters of their colonized populations.

Generally, it may be said that the legitimization of the exploitation of one group by another is tantamount to the delegitimization of any efforts on the part of the exploited group to resist its exploitation or to enjoy exactly the same privileges of their exploiters. Such efforts on the part of the exploited group will be branded as criminal or as morally reprehensible by their exploiters.

Other than the revolutionary overthrow of their exploiters or the re-possession of their political and economic resources, once thoroughly colonized and/or economically dominated, the exploited population is left with few non-self-destructive choices relative to its exploiters. A segment of the exploited population may be permitted to join their exploiters in managing their own exploitation and that of their people. Another segment of the exploited population may be permitted to work for its exploiters at comparably low wages — this while threatened by economic insecurity — and also to form a surplus labor pool. A third segment of the exploited population may seek to profit without permission or license from its exploiters. This segment, in its sickness of heart, violently feeds on itself and the exploited population, destroys the property values and unsettles the sense of security of the exploiters. Others who militantly resist exploitation are *criminalized* by their exploiters. The latter groups are singled-out for extermination or incarceration.

However, it would make an interesting thought-experiment to imagine the nature and distribution of crime and criminality were the above scenarios reversed! If the exploited populations were to regain full economic control of their lands and resources and could profit therefrom, would the crime and criminality once exported by the exploiters then return to haunt them? Would the crime and criminality in the exploited populations be measurably reduced? Are the economic/political domination and exploitation of one people by another merely benign, or are they also forms of criminalization of the exploited and de-criminalization of the exploiters?

A current and more germane issue: Does the African American community, by continuing to permit itself to be "legitimately" economically exploited by non-African American communities thereby de-legitimize itself and permit itself to be criminalized while de-criminalizing its exploiters? Has the African American community — addicted to wasteful and nonsensical consumerism, with its unwillingness to invest its wealth and human resources in itself, in America, and uncommitted to controlling its own internal markets — contributed in no small way to the criminalization of its sons, to the increasing impoverishment of its children, to the violence which prevails within its households and neighborhoods? Isn't it now time for the African American community to export the crime and criminality which were imported into it by others? How can a community which spends only *five cents* out of every dollar it earns with itself; which spends approximately 300 billion dollars with those who exploit it; 300 billion dollars which support the desires, lifestyles and standards of living of other ethnic groups — while dis-investing its own children — not encourage criminality and violence within its confines while attenuating criminality and violence in those communities it so thoughtlessly subsidizes? When the Black community squanders the economic inheritance of its own children while it fills to overflowing the coffers of the children of other communities, when it does not regulate its consummatory behavior in terms of its long-term interests — it gets the crime it deserves.

10

SUICIDE

Since suicide is a social phenomenon by virtue of its essential element, it is proper to discuss the place it occupies among other social phenomena.

— EMILE DURKHEIM
Suicide: A Study In Sociology

On superficial thought, one of the outstanding characteristics of the suicidal act is that it is illogical. Yet one can take the position that there is an implicit syllogism or argument in the suicidal act. Although we cannot be sure that our logical reconstructions of suicidal logic are correct, it remains that the suicidal person behaves *as if* he had reasoned and had come to certain — albeit, generally unacceptable — conclusions.

— E. SHNEIDMAN et al.
The Psychology Of Suicide

SUICIDE IS THE PRE-EMINENT EXPRESSION of Black-on-Black violence. It is the other side of Black-on-Black homicide. Both homicide and suicide are different forms of the collective self-destruction of a race by death. Both actualize a death-wish instigated externally, and executed internally. Both are assassinations by proxy: victim murdering victim. Both involve the killing of someone considered expendable, someone lodged between the assailant and some form of settlement or satisfaction. As in murder, in suicide there is the killer and the victim, the executioner and the executed, the judge and the condemned.

Suicide, like homicide, is dyadic. It is therefore a social act. It is the deadly vectorial outcome of a cataclysmic convergence of socially interactive forces. As in murder, in suicide killing is always done in public, in the presence of an other, whether that other is physically or mentally present and accounted for. There is always the final judgment without appeal. Someone's hopes have been unrealized, someone's vanity injured, someone's been mistreated and demands that the ultimate price be paid. Someone must be sacrificed to the needs of an other, whether that other be inside or outside the skin of the victim. Both the homicide and the suicide are victims of ideas, sacrifices made to some ideology, some system of values. Both are attempts to palliate some unbearable hurt or pain, some sickness of the soul.

The Black Family, the Black Male, and Suicide

The Eurocentric organization of American society is such that its stability depends on the dysfunctionality and near disorganization of the Black family. Infected with the germ of self-alienation, self-abnegation, self-misrepresentation, and economic deprivation, the resultant intra-familial conflict often is actualized as various forms of suicide by its young. African Americans are the most patriotic of all American ethnic groups — they sacrifice their lives every day for their country. The frequent breaking up of the African American home by many-pronged attacks on it by the racist system in which it is embedded, frequently leaves its children without a warm, caring, protective and wise parental system with which to identify and with which they can overcome an encroaching sense of emotional and social isolation: a system which can be their ally in their embattled struggle against a hostile world. For the male child the loss of his father's love and protection, or his failure to find a worthy substitute as the result of White supremacy's unrelenting and murderous assault on Black manhood, are most often the apparent stimuli which instigate his committing suicide. The chronic and overdetermined negation of African American males, if not countered by strong Black male egos, may subject them to fits of depression and dejection. These mood disorders very frequently precipitate suicidal behavior, either directly and swiftly by lethal weapons, substances, and mechanical contrivances, or indirectly and slowly by injurious addictive habits, politically-based stress, negative health practices, neglect, and reckless behavior.

The *rites of passage* through racist White American-dominated society is extremely stressful for Black youth. This is more so the case for the Black male since he receives the brunt of the White supremacist attack against Black America. Stripped of appropriate male support, guidance, protection, education, and other important coping skills by a White racist system which fears his Afrocentric competence, he is left vulnerable to the thousands of little nicks and burns, physical and psychological insults, which cumulatively push him toward self-annihilation. Not allowed the privileges and status of full and unfettered manhood by White racist male domination, a significant number of African American males are immaturized or are often led to express their "manhood" in self-destructive ways: in ways harmful to other Black males and the Black community in general. Immaturized by White racist oppression, void of overarching and long-term Afrocentric goals which provide them with maximum and healthy control over their impulses (including impulses to kill themselves) *they may commit suicide*. Without Afrocentric self-definition, possessed by an introjected alien identity, and racked by neurotic and psychotic conflict, the Black male readily becomes subject to White racist psychopolitical, psychopathological promptings and persecutions. Consequently, he may come to think that the only effective solution to his problems lie in physical or mental self-abnegation.

To be an African American male in White America is to live with anger and hostility, to feel the need to attack, to violently retaliate, to even the score. These murderous feelings without appropriate catharsis, sublimation, channeling, or targets...yet in need of outward expression...are often turned inward resulting in self-annihilation. White racist American society, harboring a poorly concealed death-wish against its Black captives, generally leaves but a few outlets for the release of societally provoked Black male rage: all inappropriate! They include the abject submission to oppression, narcosis by drugs or religion, deliberate ignorance, unending, unrewarding protests, futile *sub rosa* grumbling, overcompensatory status striving, criminality, and homicidal attacks on other Black males or on himself (suicide). Having internalized white racist values and attitudes, having been possessed by his introjected white racist demon, the suicidal African American blames his victimized self. Identified with his implanted alien spirit, he harbors a death-wish against the victims of White racist oppression amongst whom he himself is numbered. Looking at the world through jaundiced white racist eyes, he sees the enemy: And the enemy is *himself.*

Suicide Mortality of Black Males

The suicide mortality rate reaches its peak in African American males between ages twenty-five to thirty-four and in White males at age sixty-five and over.[30] Homicide and suicide are two of the leading causes of death among young Black males between ages 15 and 24. They are probably the *leading* causes if "accidental" deaths, and the many suicides on the installment plan — addictions, poor health habits, etc. — are included. Thus, Black men kill themselves with their futures ahead of them, and White men when their futures are behind them. One dies *ablossoming* in the Spring, the other after the first frosts of Autumn.

Apparently, the young African American suicide is one who has grown old while very young. He has packed all the guilt, failure, shame, fatalism, pain, hopelessness, and cynicism of a lifetime within a life-span of three decades. Somehow the cavalier optimism of youth and the willful self-confidence of young manhood are dissipated at or before the point of actualization and assumption of their powers to transform the world. Somehow Black youth and young adults are born into and come early to exist in a different and ominous reality: one that was created for them; one under the control of others. That created "reality" negates, diminishes and saps their will to live, makes their lives pointless, an absurdity filled with bitter ironies, a happenstance, a quicksand wherein every effort at self-rescue seems to pull

---

[30] U.S. Bureau of The Census, Department of Commerce, Statistical Abstracts of The U.S., 1985.

them more rapidly under, and where every branch thrown to a sinking man breaks as he struggles to reach safe ground. That created reality is the handiwork of the introjected white supremacist spirit by which the African American is possessed, with which he identifies, and with whose eyes he peers out and surveys an alien and wasted landscape which promises him no surcease and which tantalizes him with ever-receding beauteous mirages. It is that internalized Eurocentric spirit which he misidentifies as his mind and thoughts, his superego and conscience: It is those internalized racist stereotypes speaking inside his head which drive him to murder, to die, to want to be murdered in order quieten their cacophonous chorus. It is that internalized racist spirit unopposed by hope of African triumph, love of African self, self-determined competence and self-confidence and faith, which, taking possession of his body and mind, uses his own hands to take his own life.

Black-on-Black suicide is the tail face of a coin on which Black-on-Black homicide is the head face. Both are welded together by violence. Both represent violent attempts to triumph over hopelessness and despair. Both represent abject reactionary surrender to what is perceived as an immutable, oppressive ordering of the universe. While the Black-on-Black homicidal criminal seeks to triumph through the externalization of murderous aggression, the Black-on-Black suicide victim seeks to triumph through his internalization of murderous aggression. Both seek to violently cheat destiny as they have been made to see it. Their pain blinds them to other alternatives, obscures obvious, though perilous, pathways through the Valley of the Shadow of Death. Free to choose only the wrong things they both choose to murder the wrong persons for the wrong reasons.

Suicide as Displaced Aggression

Suicide is a form of displaced aggression. To internalize the white racist spirit is to internalize the White supremacist's death-wish directed at the African male. When a young Black male commits suicide it is usually a sign that the implanted White racist incubus has executed the order of its archetypal racist masters. It is the introjected white racist superego in black face which mercilessly chastises him for having sinned, and "fallen short of the glory of God" (*European man*). It is this implanted

Eurocentric conscience which threatens him with eternal damnation for having committed the *original sin* of being born African in America, which derides him for his alleged helplessness, and unworthiness: This same Eurocentric conscience tells him he will never be any good, never succeed on his own terms or otherwise, that he deserves punishment, that he is deservedly the object of hatred and revilement, that he has been cursed by God and sentenced to unending servitude, and that his death would be a favor to the world; tells him that he is unlovable, unprotected, incapable of happiness, unemployable, and that his only enemies are himself and the blackness of his skin. Having internalized the accusative self-serving conscience of his oppressors, the African American suicide victim exaggerates his self-accusation, the hopelessness of his future, his incapability for redemptive transformation. He considers his situation incorrigible. His internalized alien spirit screams its recriminations and he masochistically submits to severe feelings of guilt and self-devaluation. It is this spirit which splits his psyche into executor and executed; into the person and depersonalized, judge and condemned. Thus, when he kills he does not kill himself; he kills the "nigger" within. Through apparent Black-on-Black suicide the white supremacist establishment obscurely pushes one more African toward the *Final Solution* it plans for all Africans.

The Black victim may think that suicide represents a sort of grim triumph, a having of the last word, the last laugh on his tormentors; that his suicide represents the ultimate protest, the penultimate defiance of the will of his enemies. Suicide may be his way of refusing to live a life of quiet desperation, of masochistic screaming, and squealing supplication, while fulfilling the sadistic needs of others. Maybe, like his ancestors who voluntarily gave up the ghost during the *Middle Passage* by jumping overboard to feed the sharks, he sees living the life of a slave as not living life at all. And yet, he must know, or he quickly must be told, that such a triumph, such a hollow victory is pyrrhic, more costly to the "victor" than the vanquished; that it is an illusion of overcomance. How much more heroic to die fighting one's true enemies than to die fighting false ones; to live five minutes as a man than die forever a coward! For the fight is not against the shadows cast on the walls of one's mind but with the caster of shadows, the Wicked Witch of The West.

"For God gave us not a spirit of cowardice, but that of power and of love and of soundness of mind."[31] The power of European man over others is the power of deceit, illusion, lies and hatred over honesty, reality, truth and love. Such power *cannot* last.

---

[31] 2nd Timothy 1:7, *The New Testament Bible.*

11

COSMIC CAUSATION

An act has a past and a future; it is not contained
    within the skin of its time of occurrence
Like a rock thrown into a placid lake, its effects flow
    beyond its point of impact and ripple across
the surface of time and place unsettling things both
    near and far removed
An act is concerted; it flows from generation to
    generation into generations yet unborn
Its explosion creates a universe ever expanding; its
    throughout momentum radiating concentrically
infinity until counteracted by nullifying
    counterforces
An individual act of sin is always communal
    It is always paid for — sometimes by the sinner,
always by others; others — good and bad, righteous
    and unrighteous
For ultimately, an act of sin is impersonal
    — "it rains on the just as well as on the unjust"
"The sins of the fathers are visited unto the fourth
    generation"
The children must pay for the sins of their fathers
    for such sins are their inheritance
For they were fathered by sin
    And in accepting the bequeathed bounty of
their sinful fathers, they at one and the same time
    accept the curses of that inheritance

For with the goods of sin comes evil corrupting
　　and destroying those who would be good
For he is not truly good and innocent who eats of
　　food poisoned by sin, even if he eats them in
ignorance of their deadly nature
　　"For the wages of sin is death"
For children of evil fathers must atone the sins of
　　their fathers if they and their children and
their children's children are to escape the wrathful
　　judgment which surely must come
The sin of one is the sin of all, of the dead, of the
　　living, and of the yet to be conceived.

GOODNESS AND DECENCY under oppressive regimes are merely two versions of the same attitude — submissiveness. Law-abiding goodness and decency within the context of White American/ European socioeconomic domination involves the unresisting acceptance and self-abasing obeisance to Eurocentric values, attitudes, rules, and regulations by African Americans even when they are manifestly biased against Afrocentric interests. These forms of submissiveness ultimately involve the humble compliance with Eurocentric demands by the African American community even when such demands are exploitative, unjust, injurious, and in many instances, lethal. Eurocentrically-defined goodness and decency require that African Americans submit to White American/European domination without complaint, or that their complaints be processed through White American/European-defined "legal" channels, processed and redressed "within the system." In the name of "law and order" and "racial harmony" eurocentrically-defined goodness and decency call for the African American community to repress or compliantly restrict its just demands, to renounce or greatly attenuate their active, self-determined pursuit and fulfillment. Furthermore, they require the African American community silence its justified and valid criticisms of those who oppress and exploit it; that it defenselessly permit others to abuse it and yet to be ever ready to be indiscriminately benevolent to others, including its enemies.

　　White American/European-defined "good and decent" attitudes and behavior as internalized and practiced by African Americans are essentially quasi-religious, quasi-legalistic rationalizations and protections against anxiety, against the exaggerated fear of White American/European power; Black American/African forms of avoiding the arousal of White American/European resentment of and retaliation against African American self-determination. They also represent ways of securing reassurance by garnering European paternalistic affection. The internalization and expression of these attitudes and behaviors on the part of African Americans require they feel unworthy and incapable of goodness and decency unless defined, imposed on them, and enforced by White American/European agencies. Therefore, European/White American-defined and regulated moral/behavioral concepts are imposed against the will of the African American community without its consent and are therefore accepted by that community with a spirit of unconscious resentment, hostility, and self-loathing. These unrecognized and unacknowledged feelings then find indirect expression through projected and displaced aggressive behavior towards others — their neighbors. These feelings also find indirect expression through guilt-driven, self-destructive habits and mutually destructive social relations.

In general, the conscience implanted in the collective African American psyche is the moral/ethical agent of European/White American domination and functions to maintain that domination under the guise of mediating morally acceptable thought and behavior.

It is this implanted White American/European conscience introjected in service to White American/European domination that is rejected by the Black-on-Black criminal. It is this moral/ethical double-agent, this source of self-defeating "goodness and decency" exhibited by oppressed African Americans, which is eschewed out-of-hand by the Black-on-Black criminal. It is this externally imposed and tricky "good and decent" conscience which he so resentfully and spitefully ridicules, seeks to undermine, and finally defeats. He subliminally recognizes the sanctimonious deceit and dumb hypocrisy of those African Americans who submit to its tyrannical and exploitative demands in the name of morality, ethics, law-abidingness and brotherly love. He perceives the expediency, fear and cowardice, the weakness and absence of self-ordained authority which lurk behind their "good and decent" facades. This deception emboldens him to violate their rights and bodies, to violently assault their "innocence," to viciously pillage and plunder their properties.

This violent criminal orientation can only be sufficiently attenuated if and when the United States of America becomes a fully-liberal and egalitarian society for all, or if and when African Americans and Africans the world-over critically reject White American/European self-serving definitions of *Good and Evil* and replace these with Afrocentric/humanistic definitions and behavioral orientations.

White/European Dispensation

Often those who make laws, who discern the laws of Nature, come to think themselves as above those laws. The White American, the foremost definer, inscriber, and enforcer of laws and codes, the foremost discoverer of Nature's arcane functional infrastructure, is also their most frequent and flagrant violator, and most disingenuous subverter. And yet he feels that he should pay no penalties for their violation and subversion. Hence, his sponsorship of the most massive criminality, terror, and ecological disaster which afflicts the world today.

The White American promulgates the European regressive ethical ideology of *individual sin*; the ideological belief that a sinful act merely reflects the dysfunctionality of the person who perpetrated the act and that penalties attached to their perpetration are only to be borne by the perpetrator. This mystification permits him to deny the cosmic consequences of his own criminal behavior and to deny that he and his children must pay for violating a rule central to his ethical code — "Do unto others as you would have others do unto you" — the *Golden Rule*. Thinking himself above the law, denying its applicability to himself particularly in regard to its violation when interacting with African peoples, he assumes he may with impunity enslave, murder, rape, rob, terrorize, defraud, deceive, brutalize and do all manner of psychophysically injurious things to African peoples and escape the negative consequences of his acts. Thus he pretends undeserved and pained surprise when his dignity is insulted, his goods are "stolen," his peace disturbed, his "innocent" women and children violated, his sons assaulted, mugged and murdered, his property destroyed and devalued, and his resources wasted by some of Africa's sons. When he is cursed and reviled by those, and the children of those who he has historically and contemporaneously so heartlessly abused, he is similarly "pained and surprised." He thinks that his pillage of the resources, minds, bodies, and souls of African peoples gives him the right to sleep undisturbed, to walk the highways and byways of this earth unmolested; gives him the right to have his stolen goods be left unmolested. Yet deep in his heart he must know that the "crimes" committed against him and his children are the result of the original crimes of his fathers — his fathers, the enslavers and exploiters of the world. He must know, too, that though his fathers may have lived and died happily surrounded by their mournful slaves, that he, his children, and the children of slaves are doomed to live in enmity. Every mugging, each murder, insult, every disturbance of his peace of mind, every desecration of his property perpetrated by Black against White, every beggarly black hand thrust out by penurious Black mendicants call for reparations he must make until he chooses to retire the debts of his fathers. And he will continue to pay, as will his children, though they lifted not a whip to strike the back of a supplicating slave. For in his and their "innocence" they have not only accepted the bloody wealth and prerogatives of their fathers, but have waxed fat on their increase, and more ominously, have accepted and further cultivated the attitudes of superiority and supremacy bequeathed to them with their father's estates. Thus, "good" and "decent" White folk must suffer with the rest.

Why must these "good" and "decent" ones suffer? Because their goodness and decency are but illusions created by a repressive denial of the truth. Their innocence and goodness are the innocence and goodness purchased with stolen goods, and the blood, sweat and tears of others they fleeced of their humanity. They are allegedly good, decent and law-abiding only because through their deceptive writing and reading of history they have forgotten the murders they committed to obtain the wealth and privileges which now subsidize their "good" life. How good and decent would *White America* really be without support of its blood-money and legitimized theft of bread from the mouths of others?

The Uncivil Civilized White Man

The White American dares to think himself civilized. His "legitimate" theft of the wealth and the resources of others now "exempts" him from the need to commit "crimes in the street"; to look the people he robs and kills directly in their eyes as did his "pioneering" and colonizing fathers. With one stroke of the pen, he mugs millions and desecrates the whole of the earth. Because it is a pen he wields, and mercenary bandits he hires (including his own armed forces) to do his dirty deeds for him — and not a pistol held to the temple, a knife or a deadly grip across the throat of his victim as the Black-on-Black mugger must do — he deludes himself by thinking himself "good," "decent," and "law-abiding."

You have murdered millions of persons; plundered, pillaged and ravaged thousands of hamlets, villages, towns, cities, states and nations. Now you seek to legitimize your criminality and perceive yourself as good and law-abiding. Your civility and civilization are like the rest of your lives, purchased through the death of others. It is easy to be "law-abiding" and "decent" when you write the law and define decency and when you have the money to buy them. A true test of your ethicality would be to be good and law-abiding in the face of deliberately instigated poverty, degradation, powerlessness, hopelessness, insecurity, terror, pain and death. Until you have lived under such circumstances do you really know how "decent," "law-abiding" and "good" you really are?

Yours is a goodness born of evil. Your goodness does the work of Evil — its father. It is Evil disguised as good, hatred disguised as love. That is why your "charity" corrupts. Your "goodness" is the goodness born of not having to murder another in order to take his possessions but of having your police, your armies, mercenaries and puppet dictators do it for you. In the name of "national interests," "self-defense," "free enterprise," "private property," "fighting for democracy," "restoring peace," "maintaining the balance of power," and hundreds of other hypnotic, self-deceptive words and phrases, you hide from yourselves the murder committed by your "patriotic" sons. With diplomatic double-talk you deny that your armadas — standing and mercenary armies — your fortresses scattered hither and yond, your deadly missiles and star wars battle stations are but guns you hold to the collective temples of the world's peoples while you rob them hand-over-fist. Your newspapers and books, your media, are your instruments of repression, repressing through misrepresentation, omissions and lies the painful reality of your truly murderous trek across the globe — permitting you to think yourself inherently good and your victims inherently evil. They reverse reality, stridently screaming in their headlines about the murder of one "innocent" White victim on the streets by some "burley Black man," some "Black teen-age savages" gone "wilding," while the rape, murder and plunder of a whole African continent and its peoples does not merit a whisper in the last page, last column. Of this your "goodness" is born. And for this reason your "goodness" shall be assaulted, your peace disturbed, and you shall see evil intent staring back at you through every non-White pair of eyes. That Black man you hate and fear is the Black man you made. You are being menaced by your own shadow.

Yet there remains a question which begs an answer! While some Whites suffer the criminal depredations of Black criminals, it is Blacks who suffer far more than do Whites, from the activities Black-on-Black criminals. Why do "good and decent" Black people suffer the malice of Black criminal violence?

Victims of other people's cruelties, whether they themselves are good and decent, or evil or indecent, are not exempt from suffering for the sins of their fathers. For if fathers sell their children into bondage the children will suffer from their fathers' mercenary betrayal.

While many African ancestral fathers fought to keep their children free from enslavement, others betrayed and sold them to the White enslavers. For this betrayal, perhaps some would call it a necessary compromise, Africa's children had to pay. Slavery, colonialism, onerous subordination and general contempt, powerlessness and dependency, hunger and starvation, are but some of the crosses they have to bear for the sins of their fathers and their enslavers.

Too many of ancestral Africa's fathers and sons — forgetting the commonality of their Africanicity, differences in tribe and tradition notwithstanding — were corrupted by those who were to become their masters. They then turned on each other, and on their children, and their children turned on them. And turning around on themselves they bartered their progeny and the soul of the race for a mess of European porridge.

If the children of African American elders attack them, it is in part because their elders have betrayed them, because they have sold their children's birthright and squandered their inheritance. Black America is attacked by its children because, like too many of its slave-trading ancestral fathers, it has refused to fully recognize its fundamental Africanicity and have its constituents relate to each other and the world according to that identity. Too many African Americans have permitted the luster of gold and silver, the glitter and glamour of trinkets, status symbols and personal vanities, small comforts, false alienating ideologies and religions, the addictive pursuit of painkillers and pacifiers, the belief that Whites are invincible, to blind them to the truth and reality of what they are doing to their children.

African American mothers and fathers betray their children when in seeking to escape the anguish of their oppression, they vainly court the sympathy and love of their White American and alien exploiters. They betray their children when they, in their poverty of spirit, spend all their monies and resources to purchase their self-respect and the overpriced, shoddy goods from those who hold them in utter contempt. They delude their children when they pander to the interests of other races which are inimical to their own; and when they enrich, through trade and commerce, their oppressor's children while impoverishing their own. African mothers and fathers betray their children when they permit their oppressors to mis-educate their children.

When African American fathers choose not to prepare their sons to undertake the revolutionary overthrow of their oppressors they betray their children and the race. They thereby earn the enmity of their sons and come to live in fear of them. They see them as the enemy.

As long as African American mothers and fathers refuse to take primary responsibility for the care and welfare of their children and families; refuse to become their children's preeminent educators and enculturators; refuse to take control of their economy and bequeath their wealth to their offspring; refuse to take charge of their history and their future; refuse to accept the positive reality of their African identity and to love their African selves, they shall continue to be vindictive targets of their children's violence. And their children shall continue to be exploited and victimized by the children of alien races. And they shall continue to be victimized by indomitable addictions to euphoric substances and faddish vanities the satisfaction of which will drive them to violently victimize their brothers and sisters.

Hence, if African Americans are to be truly liberated, they must vindicate their fathers' debts by their absolute refusal to follow their fathers' erroneous ways and by dauntlessly undertaking to complete the arduous revolutionary task which, for too long, they have ignored. By these means they will forgive those ancestors who betrayed them; they will honor themselves and pay homage to those ancestors who kept the faith, fought and died that they might be free.

The race is born again in its children. Those who live today are the reincarnated ancestral spirits of those who lived yesterday. They themselves are to be the reincarnated spirits of those who will live tomorrow. Yet those who live today are more than just a link in the karmic chain which binds the generations. For by their knowledge of truth and of self, and by their courage to live true to that knowledge, they can positively transfigure their own lives, the lives of their ancestors and the lives of their progeny. Then the cycle shall be broken, the race shall be free. And once again its life shall be an example and blessing to mankind.

For every generation represents a new opportunity for a race to purify its past and to beatify its future.

12

THE NEUTRALIZATION OF
BLACK-ON-BLACK VIOLENCE

Is the contention exaggerated, or does it speak the simple
truth, that man has contrived his institutions for the
combat of crime so that he may in fact maintain it?

— PAUL REIWALD
Society And Its Criminals

THE FOREGOING DISCUSSIONS briefly outlined some of the forces
which move some African Americans toward criminality and
Black-on-Black violence. The decriminalization of the Black male
and the neutralization of Black-on-Black violence require that
we learn to discern the forces which compel Black criminal
behavior and Black-on-Black violence; that we gain an expert
knowledge of their psychopolitical, psychodynamic interaction
and of their politico-economical, socioeconomical functionality.
Decriminalization and neutralization further require that African
Americans develop, control, and effectively utilize opposing
countervailing forces against those prevailing forces which, if
permitted to continue, will extinguish African life at home and
abroad. The prevention of Black-on-Black violence and Black
criminality, which results in the incarceration of tens of thousands of young African American males in the prime of their
manhood, depends on the creation and vigorous activation of
Afrocentric countervailing forces opposed to those Eurocentric

forces which motivate and energize their criminal assault on the African American community and their self-destructive assault on themselves. These men, were their minds and bodies free, would be the leaders of the revolutionary vanguard which would overthrow and obliterate the truly criminal dominance of the European.

Afrocentric countervailing forces include: Afrocentric personal, moral, ethical values and appetitive incentives; Afrocentric cultural values, interpersonal and social interactive orientations; Afrocentric cultural motives, goals, and community organization; and Afrocentric policing, criminal justice, governance policies, and the establishment of Afrocentric economical, political, technological, cultural and military systems. The scope of this essay does not permit a discussion of the nature and purposes of each of these countervailing forces. They will be discussed in detail in forthcoming works. However, as implied by our previous analyses, the construction and effective utilization of Afrocentric countervailing forces necessary for African survival and the empowerment and enhancement of the quality of African life, require our technical understanding of a number of important facts:

1.   The continuing economical, cultural, and perhaps biological survival of African Americans and Africans the world-over, *is* in serious question. Black-on-Black violence and criminality are just two of the most salient symptoms of a people headed for self-destruction and possible annihilation. A drastic reorganization of priorities and re-examination of values: development of Afrocentric cultural, political, economic programs; and Afrocentric ethical renewal, must be undertaken if disaster is to be avoided and our survival secured. This requires a thorough understanding of the oppressive, imperialistic functioning of the ideology of Eurocentric *individualism* when it is unwittingly and unmodifiedly accepted and practiced by subordinated African peoples. Africans must recognize that "individuality" is a collective epiphenomenon that radiates from group power and prestige. There are no "individuals" who belong to powerless, degraded groups: only notorious stereotypical exceptions to a very general racist rule. Individual choice and distinction is a fringe benefit of those who belong to dominant or autonomous groups. The route to individual power is that of group empowerment. All other "individual" power is illusionary and ultimately a form of self- and other-destruction.

2.   It is of premier importance that African Americans understand the criminal, anti-life origins of White American society; understand its current national and international criminal and crimogenic nature; and how their imitation of that society — their wish to be integrated into its "mainstream," their wish to be totally identified with it; as well as their wrongheaded anger, frustration and self-alienation which result from being rejected by it; are the essential sources of Black-on-Black violence, criminality, sociopolitical and economical impotence, mental maladjustment, and racial death on the installment plan. To become one with a system which was built on African enslavement and is currently founded on the continuing socioeconomic, sociopolitical degradation, ignorance and disorganization of African peoples, is to become allied with the deadly criminal enemies of African peoples.

•   The psychodynamics of ego self-defense mechanisms, internalization of racist attitudes and perceptions, identification with the aggressor, displaced aggression, misdirected anger, rage, etc., and how they are utilized by a crimogenic Eurocentric system in its attempt to compel African Americans to engage in apparently "self-willed" acts of communal, interpersonal and individual acts of self-destruction, must be thoroughly understood. Discussions of how these mechanisms operate within the context of group power differentials must be numerous and in-depth, and the methods of counteracting their negative effects taught and trained as a part of African American education for life, survival and overcomance. The African American must come to understand that "ego self-defense," under the ineffectively opposed influence of an oppressive white racist regime, is no true defense of the ego or of the self. It is ultimately naught but a defense and rationalization of the "right" to be destructively exploited by his Eurocentric oppressors, and to join them in their annihilation of his African self.

•   Displaced aggression, which is the source of so much Black-on-Black violence, suicide and self-destructive addictive habits as well as Black educational, political, cultural and economical under-achievement, will virtually cease if African males, instead of cowering before the illusion of Eurocentric power and invincibility, would decide to stand up and make their preoccupying goal the eradication of European power and domination. They would stop killing themselves if they decide to neutralize their true frustrators, tormentors and enemies.

3.   It must be understood that it is the unexamined acceptance of the racist White American value system and the egregious imitation of White American material greed by African Americans (and Africans worldwide) which are the primary sources of Black-on-Black violence, general community disorganization, relative powerlessness and poverty. Under European domination and organization of the national and international economic systems and opportunity structures, disproportionate numbers of Africans are virtually forced to engage in the same criminal acts of violence against and oppression of African peoples as do the Europeans whose values they try so vainly to realize. In practice, the Eurocentric value system has underdeveloped African economies and impoverished African peoples, endangered the whole of life on earth, bred, aided and abetted the rape, robbery and murder of nations and peoples. Therefore the wholesale acceptance of Eurocentric values by African peoples will but hasten a destructive process that is already tidal in its immensity. A impartial examination of African values and their practical application in African life is the only means of achieving African liberation, and significantly reducing Black-on-Black violence and disintegration of the African American community. What fruits for African Americans have the tree of White American values borne?

• The African American must accept the very likely possibility that he may *never* be fully integrated as an *equal* into the so-called American mainstream. Even if he were fully accepted there is *no guarantee* that should circumstances warrant it, the Eurocentric system will not renege on its prior acceptance and eject him from the mainstream. As long as Whites possess the power of "acceptance" or "nonacceptance," the power of the purse, police, military, etc., the existence of African peoples is in jeopardy: whether integrated or segregated. African *survival* depends on meeting White power with equal or *superior* Black power. This requires the construction of an African American "nation-within-a-nation," a nation with a fully developed sociopolitical, socioeconomic system, fully invested in the ownership of the American production system to the point of obtaining an influential equity in it, and the conversion of that system from an instrument of African exploitation and death to one of African enhancement and life. Alliances between African Americans and other African nations must be forged all over the globe, and those alliances must be organized to retake control over their economic and cultural systems; the development, on the African continent and other places, of technological and scientific systems second-to-none; development of military defense systems capable of effectively defending Africans against European military incursions.

4.   The principal economic roles of African Americans in White America include those of being surplus, expendable, cheap labor and heedless consumers. These roles somewhat parallel those of Africans internationally as harvesters of basic raw materials, and as consumers of the surplus production of other nations, not as producers of finished products for their own or the consumption of others. Collectively, if the African American population were considered a nation, it would rank as the ninth or tenth richest on earth considering its national income and wealth. It would be considered one of the largest African nations in the world and with its educated and trained classes, its relatively politically sophisticated population would represent a considerable challenge to the top ranking nations on the earth today. It has developed a significant and growing coterie of administrators, bureaucrats, government officials, elected officials, civil servants, business executives, professionals, intellectuals, generals, etc., which are the foundations and sinews of a modern nation and which could represent the basis for African people to take care of and determine their own interests.

•   Yet the perception of Black America is one of poverty — material poverty and poverty of spirit. This perception which runs against the grain of African American economic reality and potential, is necessary in order to facilitate and rationalize the riotous fleecing of Black consumers and the rape of Black human and economic resources by White Americans and other ethnic groups. This rapacious exploitation of Africans requires that the Black population must starve its own members, particularly its youth, in order to support the families and youth of other ethnic groups. To meet its own economic and institutional needs, the African American population needs to spend the largest bulk of its consumer dollars with itself and engage in the production of economic goods and services which can be sold to itself and others. The African community must enter into full economic competition with other peoples. It cannot do this and continue to be the economic sucker of other peoples. Black Americans, with their very sizeable population, 12% - 15% of the general American population, and relatively large consumer wealth, spends only about five cents of each of its consumer dollars with themselves, and ninety-five cents with others. They invest relatively little of their earnings on wealth creating instruments, activities, economic organizations, and real estate. Thus, the African American community spends itself into poverty and though it possesses the capacity for tremendous economic growth and influence it does not significantly use that capacity to create employment, purpose, wealth and stability for its constituents, particularly its male members. The organization (more aptly, disorganization) of the African American economy and the psychoeconomic organization of the African American personality denies its children an economic inheritance, legacy, and tradition. Hence they become reactionarily dependent on the economic machinations of their oppressors and exploiters. The failure of the African American leadership and professional classes, petty bourgeois and business classes to appropriately organize a coherent and cohesive Afrocentric economic system, is tantamount to a rejection of their historic role and a betrayal of their people and of their children. These betrayed children are the ones which criminally assault their elders with a special hostility and vengeance. The failure of the African American middle class to invest in African economic development and empowerment is itself criminal.

•   The adult African American population must be cognizant of the fact it must earn the respect of its youth through expending its creative, organizational, and economic resources in their interest, not in the interest of the youths of other people who will one day be the enemies and exploiters of their own children. The refusal of Black America to perceive itself as a national entity (being under the influence of "American individualism") and develop an economic system and a coherent economic policy both nationally and internationally, means that it will remain psychoeconomically dependent, economically *dis*-invested, and will not be respected by other ethnic groups. Because of its refusal to invest in its economic autonomy, it cannot utilize its very considerable potential economic clout to train and employ its young men as well as to further its psychopolitical, socioeconomic interests, to insure self-defense and survival. It must build and support the social institutions necessary to determine its destiny and produce the types of children and adults who represent assets and not liabilities to its well-being. The failure of the Black community to economically invest in itself and in America, as well as to militantly utilize its consumer power to force the American economy to train and employ throughout its business strata its young men and women (while passionately seeking to imitate White American consumption patterns and engage in compensatory, conspicuous consumption) potently encourages Black male criminality, Black-on-Black violence, drug addiction, family disorganization, intellectual retardation, general communal disintegration and demise.

5. A people, and a nation, is created, re-created, and sustained through the appropriate education and training of its youth. Every culture engages in some form of education and training, the principal function of which is to secure cultural identity, continuity, organization, integrity and above all, survival. When a people is miseducated or inappropriately educated and trained, its sense of peoplehood is destabilized as is concomitantly its individual and collective psyches, and its capacity to withstand the deadly assaults and exploitative pillaging by other peoples and the insidious wasting away of its vitality.

African Americans are educated and trained to further the imperial and exploitative interests of racist White America — interests inimical to their own. They are therefore educated against their own interests, which is one of the reasons that despite their sizeable educated, professional and trained classes relative to other nations, their economic and political power is benign and their survival is in question. Black-on-Black violence, criminality, social dysfunctionality, economic instability, defensive vulnerability, can to a great extent be traced back to African

Americans not understanding the basic function of education and of educational institutions, and permitting their exploiters and oppressors to determine the nature of the educational experience of their children. Consequently, when African Americans are educated and trained under white racist domination — no matter how highly educated or how highly trained — they are educated to serve the predominant needs of their White oppressors and thus trained for servitude. Those left untrained, uneducated, undereducated, miseducated and unemployed, also are made so at the pleasure of White America. Ultimately, a certain type of ignorance and ineptitude, a certain dumbness, regardless of level of formal education or the lack of it, is maintained among African Americans and Africans in general. It is by means of this fundamental dumbness that Eurocentric domination and exploitation are efficiently maintained and remain unchallenged.

When educated through the auspices of their exploiters, African Americans and Africans in general are educated into ignorance, are made the recipients of an alienated education which means that it can be utilized only to further alien interests. Thus, the formal and informal education of African American youth is an education in alienation, self-abnegation, incompetence, unreality and wrongheadedness. Many of the youth, particularly the males, resist this alienating, anti-life, emasculating and insulting process: a process designed to prepare them for subordinate places in a racist society. They reject and refuse to cooperate with this design, and through "antisocial" acts offend, tax the resources of, and attack its perpetrators. They defend valiantly, though self-destructively, what shreds of "masculinity" they have left. They violently attack the elders and the community who and which have failed to educate them around African cultural identity and purpose, independence, self-determination, responsibility, self-knowledge and self-love: education for the attainment of a fulfilling and liberated life. If African American youth are to be educated away from their "antisocial" proclivities and educated in ways that permit them to legitimately actualize their human potential and secure the biological and cultural survival of African peoples, they must be educated, especially during their impressionable years, by their own elders and equipped with an Afrocentric education. Suffice it to say that if the education of African youth is designed to primarily serve the interests of African peoples and to maintain the wholesome integrity of the African community, such education must be grounded in objective analyses of the African psychohistorical and psychocultural experience as well as African future development.

Today the education of African children is one in search of a considered Afrocentric pedagogic theory. The overarching goal and function of education must be that of seeking to insure the survival of a people, to enhance their quality of life, their ability to exercise self-determination and a self-created sense of peoplehood, personhood, and humanity. African youth must be educated to carry out the revolutionary overthrow of their oppressors. An appropriate education and training of African American youth must take into consideration the transformation and distortion of the African personality and psyche, and the resulting distortion of their cognitive, emotional, and behavioral characteristics which have taken place and continue to take place under European oppression. The African American community must grasp that it has to train its young to accomplish tasks which are diametrically opposed to those of White American youth. Consequently, there can be no such thing as *equal* education, the *same* education, provided to both African American and White American youth. The education of African American youth must be measured according to the *standards* and *needs* of African peoples if those peoples are to leave the path leading to self-destruction. The beneficial education of Black youth and the African American population can only occur within the confines, and under the control of, African American communities and institutions. The education of African American males must occur in African American homes, churches, private schools, preempted public schools, auditoriums, prisons, and any other places where the truth and reality of the African history, experience and destiny can be taught; where their teachers, their people, have a profound understanding of the developmental psychology of the African American child, a knowledge of the tasks they must accomplish, and can train them in how to accomplish those tasks.

The appropriate rearing and education of African American children require that African American people recognize the inappropriateness of White American parenting and pedagogical approaches for their children. They require that African

Americans review the pragmatic approaches to child rearing and socioeconomic organization utilized by their ancestors, and the creation and adaptation of new approaches where necessary. For example, the African American acceptance of the European family model as representing the ideal and valid model for their own family organization, despite the markedly different psycho-economical, psychohistorical origins and contemporary contexts of the European family configuration relative to that of the African American family configuration, has resulted in the perception of the predominantly African American family configuration as deviant, deficient and pathological. For instance, the African American's acceptance of the Eurocentric conception of the father's role in the family as the primary and only male responsible for the training for manhood and adulthood of his sons has crippled Black America's capacity to creatively train its sons for manhood and adulthood when nearly half of its families are femaleheaded. A review of their ancestral history would teach them that the training of male youth is a community activity: a responsibility of communal males, not just that of the biological father. Thus, the absence or ineptness of the biological African father would not necessarily have the negative ramifications it has in contemporary Black America. A radical redefinition of manhood and fatherhood, of training for manhood, must be undertaken by the African community in America if its youth is to be saved, the prisons are to be emptied of its men, the community is to decriminalize itself, defuse Black-on-Black violence, and create a just, harmonious, secure, and prosperous African American people.

Why Crime Prevention and Rehabilitative Programs Fail

Since White America maintains its positive collective self-concept and rationalizes its oppression of its African population by projectively degrading all things African, it cannot be expected that it will promulgate effective crime prevention programs. It cannot negate that upon which its psychopolitical, psycho-economical life depends. Its pressing need to perceive African Americans, particularly African American males, as innately criminal, requires that it perceives them as incorrigible and incapable of rehabilitation. These perceptions, whether held consciously and/or unconsciously, mean that crime prevention, rehabilitation, and other programs and approaches designed to prevent crime in the Black community or to significantly reduce Black recidivism, when controlled by Whites, and rationalized on the basis of White psychology, are doomed to fail through self-defeat. Moreover, White American crime prevention and rehabilitative methods, because of White ambivalence toward alleged Black criminality and Black-on-Black violence, tend to help increase, or at best not effectively reduce, Black criminality. Hence, eurocentrically oriented corrections facilities and criminal justice systems are often "schools for crime."

It must be acknowledged that the continuing European need to dominate and economically exploit African peoples requires that inequities of power and privilege persist and be enforced between the supreme Europeans and the subordinate Africans. Ultimately, this implies that fairness and parity under these circumstances cannot operatively exist between Blacks and Whites. A White dominated and rationalized criminal justice system, for the foregoing reasons, must be unjust, particularly in regard to African American males. White America's need to dominate Blacks means that every White American institution must operate in opposition to its implied mission and name when dealing with African peoples. Thus the criminal justice system must produce injustice; the corrections system must promote *incorrection* — just as the Eurocentric economic system must impoverish Africans.

Thus, when the White American criminal justice establishment talks about crime prevention it really speaks to the issue of how African Americans can be contained or kept in their "places" and prevented from escaping. Its chief concern is with African American containment and the prevention of White victimization by Black criminals. It is far from being passionately concerned about the prevention and reduction of Black-on-Black violence and Black criminal victimization of the African American community. This establishment is one with all other Eurocentric institutional establishments in that they all function to maintain White supremacy and in service to that purpose, to maintain Black communal destabilization, or Black communal stabilization at the price of having Blacks humbly accept (in a moral/religious, intellectual, emotional, and behavioral sense), the "places" chosen for them by their Eurocentric oppressors. As we have intimated, White America needs Black criminality to maintain its illusory positive self-image and politicoeconomic hegemony. It profits economically in many ways from the processing of Black males through its criminal justice and corrections systems and its crime prevention and rehabilitative programs. In place of ineffective rehabilitative programs and the necessary restructuring of American society, it stridently demands more draconian police methods; the continuing erosion and abridgement of African human and civil rights; an increasing emphasis on preventative detention; construction of more and larger prisons; longer and harsher sentencing of alleged convicts (especially Black ones); increasingly treating Black youthful offenders as adult offenders; defunding and rendering ineffective rehabilitative programs and services such as family counseling, probation and parole; as well as effectively neutering proven rehabilitative approaches and new experimental rehabilitative techniques.

Frankly, the most effective means for reducing Black criminality and Black-on-Black violence would be the prevention, correction, and rehabilitation, not of Black criminals, but of fundamental White racist criminality, White-on-Black violence, both psychical and physical, and the pathology of White racism. Black American crime is the progeny of White American criminal intercourse with African people. But since this course of action is very unlikely to be followed, it is necessary that the African American community successfully undertake its own prevention, correction and rehabilitative programs. It must take *history* into its own hands. While we have stressed the production of Black criminality by White criminality, this does not imply that Black criminality and Black-on-Black violence can only cease when White America decides that White-on-Black violence should cease. This does not imply that African Americans are not to some measurable extent, responsible for the phenomena of Black criminality and Black-on-Black violence or that the African American community does not possess the internal, autonomous means of significantly reducing and preventing its victimization by Black criminals and violence-prone offenders. In fact, the surest way of ridding American society and the world of crimogenic Eurocentric dominance, imperialism and exploitation, is for the African American community to refuse to let sizable numbers of its constituents to be reactionarily tempted into criminal, violent and self-destructive behavior or to tolerate or justify its existence. To a significant extent, White America is the reciprocal creation of Black America: Whites cannot be what they are unless Blacks choose to be or accept what they are. The relationship between White and Black America is both a parasitic and symbiotic one: a change in one necessitates a change in the other. And the African American community is capable of self-determined, autonomous change!

The premise of this essay is that to a very significant extent Black criminality and Black-on-Black violence are reactionary forms of behavior. This implies that if the African American community is to rid itself of reactionary Black criminality, it must expunge from its collective personality and psyche its tendency to respond to White racist provocation of various types and in stimulus-bound reactionary ways. It must learn not to react unthinkingly and self-defeatedly to White racist insults to the collective African ego complex. It must learn to resist White American material, social, economic, cultural enticements and seductions. How Black America chooses to react to the actions of White America determine the psychosocial, psycho-economical, psychopolitical influence and outcome of those White American actions, regardless of their original intentions. If it chooses to gain control of its own mental, emotional, behavioral and material processes, define and regulate its own institutional systems, then the African American community must determine the quality of its own community life to captain its own ship and determine its own destiny.

The earnest rehabilitation of the Black-on-Black criminal must begin with the acknowledgment that such a process must be one with full liberation of the African community and African peoples worldwide. The alienation of the individual African is endemically reflective of the alienation of the African community. A community is its people. Its oppression requires the concrete oppression of the persons who constitute it. Its permanent oppression, subordination, and exploitation requires that its individual constituents and the social relations which inhere between them, be organized and simultaneously disorganized in a way such that its autonomous and wholesome existence should never be actualized. This is the fundamental condition upon which enduring European/White American political-economical hegemony and White supremacy uneasily rests. Thus, the mental and socioeconomical maladaptiveness of African individuals and peoples and their social relations is a political-economic necessity if today's ethnocultural status quo is to be preserved intact. It follows then that the African American and African peoples in general must be subjected to a deliberate and efficient program of White American/European created and sustained socioeconomic/cultural destablization paradigms. These paradigms are reflected in the destablization, confusion, alienated adjustment and self-destructiveness of many African communities and nations.

Any serious "rehabilitation" program dealing with African individuals and groups must be founded on the knowledge that the continuance of White American/European domination of African peoples requires continued African mental and social maladaptiveness. The social and individual ills that plague the African American community are politically inspired. Therefore, their rehabilitation must be politically informed and understood as a form of political activism, the goals of which must include the overthrow and permanent disablement of White supremacy, the root cause of those ills to begin with. The appropriate treatment of the Black-on-Black criminal must, by the very casual nature of his ailments, include his psychopolitical deprogramming and reconstruction. His aggressive impulses must be redirected. They must be given their appropriate definition, causes and objectives, including above all, the liberation of his African self, of African peoples, and the ending of White supremacist global hegemony. To accomplish these ends he must not only understand the social psychological and psychodynamic sources of his violent behavior. He must be educated in the arts of self-control, social organization, cooperation, creative-strategic thinking and behavior, self-love, self-acceptance, and love of his people.

Black Perceptions of White Law Enforcement

The contradictions discussed above are further complicated by the fact that many African Americans justifiably perceive the police force principally as an alien, hostile, colonial/imperialistic constabulary deployed against them. The force's reasons for being in the African American community is seen as that of maintaining the racist status quo through intimidation of the local Black populace, reinforcing stereotypical racist attitudes, prerogatives, and power, protection of property (*particularly that owned by alien landlords and merchants*), rather than people. It appears more concerned with containing crime within the African American community rather than preventing it. Many African American communities suspect the police of *corruptly* cooperating with certain criminal elements, particularly drug dealers and petty racketeers, of being "on the pad" to those elements as well as sponsoring those elements directly thereby abetting the criminality they are allegedly there to eradicate.

When police personnel demonstrate racist contempt for the people, they are supposed to protect — whose servants they are supposed to be — it is not difficult to imagine their lack of zealous and unbiased enforcement of the laws. A racist police force is vulnerable to corruption by local criminals whose activities are seen by it as only impacting on a race and population they care very little for, if not hate: a race and population they view as essentially subhuman, criminal, and not worthy of respect. Under these circumstances the police and the African American community perceive each other as the enemy. Their relationship becomes characterized by acrimony and mutual distrust.

For many African Americans the police are "the law." Police and the laws they are supposed to enforce are synonymous. When the police arbitrarily and along racist lines, enforce or ignore the laws, when they personalize law enforcement or violate the letter and spirit of the laws they are supposed to uphold, the populace loses respect for the police and the law. Viewing the police and "the law" as one and the same means that loss of respect for the police is synonymous to loss of respect for "the law." If the police are held in contempt, so are the laws they ostensibly represent or with which they are associated.

The laws will not be respected merely because they have been approved by the appropriate societal institutions and according to constitutional procedures. To be effectively respected they must be perceived as morally correct, honestly motivated, as not designed to protect and rationalize racial and/or class privilege and power, and enforced without bias. This has not been the case in regard to the laws and law enforcement relative to African Americans. African Americans have seen the laws and the law enforcement establishment be used to deny them their constitutional, civil and human rights. They have seen "the law" and its enforcers take sides with reactionary White American communities and join with those communities in hypocritically and blatantly violating their own legal and moral codes to maintain racial advantages. Not only has the African American community suffered emotionally from the violations by Whites of their own moral and legal codes; they have witnessed the writing and enforcement of laws which are specifically designed and passed to facilitate their domination and exploitation, their humiliation and degradation, their subordination and dehumanization, by the White American community. This historical and contemporary situation has bred contempt for laws and authorities, for social mores and etiquette, and motivated open, rebellious subversion of these entities by certain relatively small but influential elements of the African American community. It has reinforced criminal contempt and activity in many youth and young adults because of the pleasure derived from outwitting the laws and their enforcers, laws promulgated and enforced by outsiders and enemies and therefore only to be obeyed by "squares" and "chumps." Prestige is thereby gained in the eyes of unsophisticated Black youth by Black-on-Black criminals who in their perverted ways dare to challenge racist White supremacy as represented by the laws and authorities, even if such unthinking subversion, resistance and rebellion may ultimately prove to be self-defeating, self-destructive, wrongheaded and pointless.

The African American Community and Improved Law Enforcement

The following conditions must inhere if the African American community, in cooperation with the law enforcement and criminal justice establishments, is to commit itself effectively to the support of the nation's laws, their enforcement, and is to prevent or significantly reduce criminal activity in its midst:

- The laws must be rigorously and equitably enforced and not purposely, or in effect, written to rationalize and protect race or class prerogatives and power advantages.

- The laws must be consonant with generally accepted moral, valuational and constitutional preachments and written with the mutual agreement of the people — including the African American people.

• Law enforcement establishments, authorities, and personnel must impartially enforce the laws and not permit themselves to be perceived as representatives and enforcers of discriminatory racial, class, institutional attitudes and practices.

• Law enforcement personnel should reflect the ethnic compositions of the African American communities they serve, and should employ at all levels a representative number of African American personnel who possess a high level of Afrocentric consciousness and demeanor. Those police units which operate within the African American community, the cities and highways in general, should possess a sound working knowledge of the culture, history, and behavioral character of the African American community and demonstrate an earnest respect for it.

• Police personnel should be taught to perceive and acquit themselves not as occupiers of the African American community, not as its rulers or as enforcers of quasi-colonial laws but as its servants, employees, as its representatives, and who along with the members of that community are mutually and co-equally concerned and involved in protecting its best interests.

• Police and criminal justice personnel responsible for violating the rules of common decency and courtesy, for the use of racial slurs and epithets, for abuse of power and authority, the use of unnecessary force, other forms of harassment and injurious behavior when dealing with African American citizens, should be visited with certain, swift, and effective chastisement.

• Police authorities and personnel must be equally and as speedily responsive to the needs of the African American community as they are to non-African American communities.

- Police personnel and authorities must serve and learn to differentiate the criminal and noncriminal elements in the African American community, and be perceived as even-handedly opposed to its criminal elements and as zealously protective of its citizens' lives and properties, as respective of their rights and humanity as they are the criminal elements, lives, properties, rights and humanity of other ethnic communities.

- The police and criminal justice establishments must respect the intelligence of the African American community and exhibit full confidence in its capacity to know how best to solve its social problems. They, therefore, should be prepared to actively listen to the community and diligently support its efforts, not paternalistically and autocratically dictate solutions to its problems.

- The African American community should by all means saliently demand the swift, sure and effective punishment of those of its constituents who dare victimize, in whatever manner and for whatever reasons, any other of its members. Culprits who commit Black-on-Black crime should be aware of the fact that the community will not tolerate, rationalize, countenance or in any way condone (historical racism as a causal factor notwithstanding) the victimization of one Black by another. The African American community must rid itself of the internalized racist belief that African life is less precious than non-African life, especially White life. Having done this and having actively committed itself to the revolutionizing of the police and criminal justice establishments along the lines suggested above, as well as having committed itself to its full internal socioeconomic, sociocultural, psychopolitical reorganization, the African American community must unequivocally and loudly condemn, and vigorously pursue the fair-minded prosecution of those Blacks who harm other Blacks, no matter their station in life.

Recommendations for African American Community Preservation and Empowerment

The African American community must realize that it has the *right* and duty to defend itself from its criminal elements if the government, to which it pays taxes, and whose officials it helps to elect, fails to do so. The ability of *unarmed* Black Muslim young men and of other Black community organizations — with or without police support — to successfully neutralize or markedly reduce criminal activity from some African American neighborhoods throughout the U.S.A., demonstrates clearly the African American community's potential for ridding itself of crime if encouraged and organized to do so.

For approximately one-third of what a city like New York City expends to employ its patrol forces, a comparable group of young African American males and females could be trained and stipendiated to patrol and protect their own communities. While White America utilizes its sons and daughters to provide protection for itself (which is the police establishment's principal function) the African American community is not permitted to exercise that right, hence its occupation by colonial police forces. Policing their communities would provide very valuable opportunities for teaching young African American males that their first duty is the protection of their people against internal and external victimization. The opportunity to develop discipline, work habits, appropriate attitudes toward and relationships with authority, to learn to appreciate order, to learn to command as well as to obey, is lost when the African American community is treated as some dependent, defenseless, neocolonial protectorate by the White American-controlled constabulary.

Finally, the fear that African American and the worldwide African communities may develop their own effective internal authority system, their own autonomous *afrocentrically* based organization, which could place them in the position to challenge the hegemonic White American national and global White American/European socioeconomic systems, motivates those sociopolitical conglomerates to actively oppose any semblance of African American self-determination and self-defense. For when all is told, Black self-defense and self-determination is viewed by Whites as criminal offenses and as threats to White authority. Thus, in the defense of its authority, the White community promotes the defenselessness of the Black community against its own self-destruction. The African American community — at the expense of having to confront the White American community, the White-dominated police force and criminal justice establishment — must not let this situation continue if it is to survive and prosper.

Prevention of Black-on-Black criminality and violence through more rational law enforcement, through the unbiased execution of appropriate criminal justice procedures and the provision of effective counseling and rehabilitation services, is not the same as the prevention of Black-on-Black criminality and violence through the Afrocentric organization of the African American community. While law enforcement and criminal justice systems may effectively suppress, thwart or correct criminal tendencies, intent, and activity *after* they occur, and may reduce crime in one area by deflecting it to another, appropriate socialization of children, equitable and fair organization and distribution of national and community resources, the provision of Afrocentric educational training and of equitable occupational opportunities, can suppress and redirect possible criminal tendencies, and activities *before* they are actualized or can occur. Crime prevention would then result from internal, personal and communal processes rather than from the exertion of external, alien and ultimately corrupting, constabulary forces. To accomplish this end the African American community must:

- Recapture its Afrocentric self. For it is with the "splitting off" of the African American ego complex from its African self that the tragic transformation of too many Africans into antisocial personalities begin to take place. Neurotic and psychotic behavior is essentially measured by the degree to which the individual is out of touch with reality; the more out of touch with his sociohistorical reality, the more neurotic, psychotic, maladjusted and/or self-destructive. The African American community must confront and accept the reality of its African cultural origins — and identity. The rejection of this reality is the acceptance of psychopathology.

- Rebuild, re-create, and create African based cultural and moral values essential to the regaining the cultural sanity, health, liberation, and survival of the African American and Pan-African communities.

- Build Afrocentric national and international economic, military, technological and political systems not dependent on European consent. African power must originate from the psychopolitical heart of African peoples.

- Take full responsibility for providing its children with an Afrocentric education based on Afrocentric psychology and pedagogic techniques designed to serve the survival and life-enhancement needs of African peoples. The community must take over caring for the health and welfare of its constituents through the increase and distribution of its own wealth and through the vigorous exertion of its collective political power and influence in the U.S.A. Accepting continuing charity from outsiders corrupts the spirit and health of a people.

- Take the initiative and responsibility for building and providing adequate housing and employment for its constituents.

- Make one of its central motivating goals the overthrow of European and Eurocentric (and any other ethnocultural group's), psychopolitical, psychocultural, socioeconomic, techno-military, religio-ethical domination of African peoples. This decrees that the African American community envision itself as a people — a nationality — as a nation-within-a-nation, organize and function as such, and relate to the other pluralistic ethnocultural groups as such. For in reality, the African American community is perceived and treated as a separate, outlaw, outcast nation. The refusal to deal with the reality of its separateness and use it to its own advantage, to accept the reality of the pluralistic organization of America society where each ethnocultural group is almost exclusively concerned with its own welfare, entering alliances and coalitions when it is to their advantage to do so, are the sources of the African American community's current negative and frightening vulnerability to alien economic exploitation and to self-destruction. The survival of African American communities cannot continue to be based on the fickle "largesse" and "moral turpitude," "sympathy," "empathy" and "brotherly love" of the White American community.

- Take its destiny into its own hands. The African American community must psychosocially be "born again." It must rehabilitate its incarcerated population and itself by getting to know its true ancient, pre-enslavement, enslavement, and contemporary history; by getting to know the true history and psychology of its oppressors and of other peoples; by getting to know how it was and is created and manipulated in service of Eurocentric and European interests and, conversely, against its own. It must recognize that it is possessed by an antagonistic eurocentrically introjected spirit, a spirit with which it self-destructively identifies and over which it has little or no control, and which directs its collective personality in opposition to its true purpose and character. It must recognize that everything originates out of a psychopolitical milieu, possesses psychopolitical purposes, has psychopolitical implications, emanations, effects and ramifications. The understanding of these phenomena and their application to the reconstruction of the African American community, to correcting the incarcerated African American population, to the rearing, guidance, education and counseling of African American children, will provide an indestructible foundation upon which African liberation and the liberation of humankind can be re-constructed and realized.   ■

EPILOGUE

WHY DO WE SPEAK OF REVOLUTION? That word which portends cataclysmic change and overthrow; the changing of the order of things! *"Why?,"* we ask ourselves, we, African Americans, must speak of revolution at this day and time:

> *When peace and freedom are breaking out*
> *all over the Russia(s) and the Balkans.*
> *And the spirit of unity sweeps like a refreshing breeze*
> *across Western Europe and the divided Germanies.*
> *When in South Africa, Mandela throws away his shackles;*
> *When in North America there is no longer the color line;*
> *When Jessie runs for President, Colin Powell marshals*
> *the world's mightiest war machine.*

> *A land where Dinkins, Jackson, Goode, Young, James,*
> *Schmoke, Bradley, rule great cities;*
> *Where Wilder governs a great state;*
> *Where African men and women as ministers*
> *sit in presidential cabinets, don robes of Justice,*
> *and take their places on the boards of directors*
> *of America's global corporations —*
> *Where Reginald Lewis places TLC on the Fortune 500.*

Why not speak of brotherhood and of joining hands? Of dreams? Or least keep silent and not cause undue alarm...and let those who are going for a swim in the mainstream rush headlong, unimpeded by the call to War?

I speak of revolution. I beat the drums of war because no one man, nor a few famous men, are a people. The rule of one, the judgeship, the generalship, the ministry, the captaincy of industry of one, of a few, is not the rulership of the people. The life of a few heroes and heroines is not the life of a people.

I speak of revolution because we are yet to have one. Our freedom and liberation are yet to be won and secured. Our enemies still rule us and their numbers increase. Their strength grows exponentially.

In our revelry, inebriated by our celebration of ephemeral victories we have left our borders unwatched. Our sentinels sleep at their posts. The enemy stealthily infiltrates our camps and prepares to slaughter us before we wake! For peace and unity among our enemy are joined to disturb and to make impossible our own.

We spoke easily of revolution in the 60s and 70s. We shouted from mountaintops and deep valleys — Black Power! We raised our clenched fists toward the sky as if to threaten the heavenly hosts — and vowed to march on till victory is won! Is victory won the reason we no longer sing our battle hymns; we no longer study war; we have retired our uniforms and fallen from our militant formations?

As we lift every voice and sing hosannas
And loudly give all praises due to our ancestors
To our heroes past and present
As African men and women aspire to the highest offices
And win seats at the table of the mighty
The heroes and heroines of our future
The futures of our people
The carriers of our ethnic immortality
Our young warriors, the mothers of our nation,
The minds or our race fall
Like wheat before the sharpened sickle of crack,
dope, and AIDS
They are slain in the wombs of our mothers
Their minds are terribly wasted in the schools
mastered by their enemies
They kill each other pulling the triggers of guns
they cannot even manufacture
Their lives go up in smoke

A mayor of the nation's capital falls from his pedestal. Does our salvation lie in being elected?

In this the winter of our discontent, the written word is still perceived as an unintelligible cryptic hieroglyph. To many of our children basic mathematics still presents unsolvable riddles. Knowledge of self-love, self-confidence, and doing for self are still Holy Grails yet to be attained.

While a few attain wealth, the multitudes slip desperately into poverty, sickness and disease — their life-span shrinking faster than their horizons.

Flashback:

THE NEW YORK TIMES
OUAGADOUGOU, BURKINA FASO, JANUARY 29, 1990
Pope John Paul arrived today in this struggling land and begged the affluent nations "not to scorn" Africa's hungry millions.

"How," he pleads, "would history judge a generation that having all the means to feed the world's population, refused to do so with fratricidal indifferences?

"The earth is becoming sterile across an immense area, malnutrition is chronic in tens of millions of people, too many die," he cried. "Is it possible that such a need is not felt by all humanity?"

Is it possible, I say, that a people who complacently watch my African Brothers perish; who help them along their path of death; would not kill me also? I am an African. The death of my brother is also my death!

Flashback:

THE TIMES, JANUARY 16, 1990. WASHINGTON.
For the senior officers who serve time as instructors at the nation's top level military schools, teaching what they know is no longer enough.... Now they find that the threat from the Soviet Union in growing more ambiguous by the day and say that war-games portraying the Soviet Union as the aggressor are increasingly irrelevant.

"The threat is no longer the Russians," said Captain John N. Heidt of the Navy school. "The threat is uncertainty." "The Russians are 'out' and the Third World is 'in'," said Lieutenant Col. Paul Pugh.

For the tyrant still sits on the throne
His reign of terror like a wind-blown wildfire
Sweeps across the cities towns and villages
Crackles the trees of the forest
Incinerates the farmlands of our people

He is the tyrant of a thousand faces
All of them we know
Sometimes they smile
Sometimes they frown
Sometimes they are serious
Sometimes they clown

Sometimes they tell we are slaves
Other times they say we are free!
But the one thing they try to keep from us
Is that they're all one face
The face of White Supremacy!

And many in this land of plenty have no home; like the son of man — nowhere to lay their bones. Black men rot in jail; their unfathered sons die in the streets; their daughters sell their souls to the highest bidders; their children rearing children; their people regressing instead of progressing.

Flashback:

BUSINESS WEEK: SEPTEMBER 19, 1988

The cover screams:
Human capital: The Decline of America's Work Force

It whispers:
And as the economy comes to depend more and more on women and minorities, we face the massive job of education and training.

It wonders:
"Can they be taught?"

It proposes:
Let's import new immigrants educated and trained to do the job.

THE NEW YORK TIMES: JULY 26, 1989
Blacks Found Lagging Despite Gains
The National Research Council, arm of the National Academy of Sciences and Engineering reports: Racial Discrimination is only one of several major barriers to improvements for the nation's 30 million Blacks.

"Full integration of blacks into a 'color blind' society is unlikely in any foreseeable future," largely because of existing social and economic separation they say. If all racial discrimination were abolished today, the life prospects facing many poor blacks would still constitute major challenges for public policy.

Is the American Dream becoming a Nightmare?

The Chairman of Xerox Corporation calls it "the making of a National disaster." Former chairman of the Procter and Gamble Company fears the creation of "a third world within our own country."
The *New York Times* went on to warn:

...the students who are most at risk are children from minority groups — the same youngsters who fill 56% of the new jobs that will open up between 1986 and the year 2000.
America is developing into a nation of educational haves and have-nots; who are becoming employment haves and have-nots; polarization follows racial lines, and...the effect on the economy and the country can be devastating.

Is this the Promised Land our Prophet saw from the Mountain Top?

Flashback:
NEWSWEEK, FEBRUARY, 22, 1988: $2.00
Special Report: The Pacific Century:
"Is America In Decline?"

I ask: Is the mainstream drying up? Somewhat more ponderously, I ask: Are we to remove the foot of White racism from our necks to have it replaced by that of the Asian economic juggernaut?

Why do I speak of Revolution? Our people are dying. Our people are yet downtrodden near the level of the ground. It must be revolution or it will be death. And I intend to live! Don't you?

■

BIBLIOGRAPHY

America Friends Service Committee, *Struggle for Justice*. New York: Hill and Wang, 1971.

Bandura, Albert. *Principles of Behavior Modifications*. New York: Holt, Rinehart & Winston, Inc., 1969.

Brown, Lee. National Urban League *The State Of Black America 1988*.

Chorover, S. *From Genesis to Genocide: The Meaning of Human Nature and the Power of Behavior Control*. Cambridge, Mass: MIT Press, 1980.

Cloward, R. & Ohlin, L. *Delinquency and Opportunity*. New York: The Free Press, 1965.

Coser, L. *Continuities in the Study of Social Conflict*. New York: The Free Press, 1967.

Deleuze, S. & Guatarri. *Anti-Oedipus: Capitalism and Schizophrenia*. Minneapolis: University of Minnesota, 1983.

Durkheim, Emile. *Suicide: A Study in Sociology*. New York: The Free Press, 1951.

Fenichel, Otto. *The Psychoanalytical Theory of Neurosis*. New York: W. W. Norton, 1945.

Fredrickson, George. *White Supremacy. A Comparative Study in American and South African History*. New York: Oxford University Press, 1981.

Freire, Paulo. *Pedagogy of the Oppressed*. New York: Continuum, 1983.

Hansbury, Lorraine. *A Raisin in the Sun*. New York: Random House, 1969.

Hartjen, Clayton A. *Crime and Criminalization*. 2nd ed., New York: Prager Publishers, 1978.

Horney, Karen, *Neurosis and Human Growth: The Struggle Toward Self-Realization*. New York: W.W. Norton, 1950.

_____ , *Our Inner Conflicts: A Constructive Theory of Neurosis*. New York: Norton, 1966.

Jordan, Wintrop. *White Over Black: American Attitudes Toward the Negro, 1550-1882*. Chapel Hill: North Carolina Press, 1968.

Kovel, Joel. *White Racism: A Psychohistory*. New York: Columbia University Press, 1984.

Lewis, Michael. *The Culture of Inequality*. New York: New American Library, 1978.

Lowen, Alexander. *The Betrayal of the Body*. New York: Collier, 1967.

May, Rollo, *Power or Innocence: A Search for the Sources of Violence*. New York: W.W. Norton, 1972.

Menninger, Karl, *Man Against Himself*. New York: Harcourt, Brace, Jovanovich, 1938.

Parenti, M. *Democracy for the Few*. 5th ed. New York: St. Martin, 1987.

Platt, Tony. *Prospects for a Radical Criminology in the United States*.

Reinwald, Paul. trans. & ed. by James, J.E. *Society and Its Criminals*. London: Heineman, 1949.

Ryan, William. *Blaming the Victim*. New York: Random House, 1971.

Schur, Edwin M. *Our Criminal Society: The Social and Legal Sources of Crime in America*. New Jersey: Prentice Hall, 1969.

Shapiro, David. *Neurotic Styles*. New York: Basic Books, 1965.

Shneidman, E. et al. *The Psychology of Suicide*. New York: Science House, 1970.

Slater, Philip. *The Pursuit of Loneliness: American Culture at the Breaking Point*. Revised ed. Boston: Beacon Press, 1976.

Swomley, J.M., Jr. *American Empire: The Political Ethics of Twentieth-Century Conquest*. New York: Macmillan, 1970.

Walker, E. & Heyns, R. *An Anatomy of Conformity*. New Jersey: Prentice Hall, 1962.

Watzlawick, P., ed., *The Invented Reality: How Do We Know What We Believe We Know?* New York: W. W. Norton, 1984.

Wellman, D. *Portraits of White Racism*. Cambridge: Cambridge University Press, 1977.

Wolff, R., ed. *The Sociology of George Simmel*. New York: MacMillan 1950.

Index